The
Perfect
Man®

The Perfect Man®

Created by

Dean and Merril Buckhorn

Andrews McMeel
Publishing

Kansas City

01 02 03 04 05   KWF   10 9 8 7 6 5 4 3 2 1

ISBN: 0-7407-2237-9

BOOK COMPOSITION BY KELLY & COMPANY

The
Perfect
Man®

The Perfect Man.

(He's tall. He's happy.
And he's a lot more stable
than all the other flakes.)

The Perfect Man.

(He's cute. He's colorful. And his old girlfriends are a billion miles away.)

The Perfect Man.

(He's strong. He's simple.
And he knows the perfect way
to top off a long day.)

The Perfect Man.

(He's sweet. He's smooth. And if you need a friend, you can chew his ear off.)

The Perfect Man.

(He's cute. He's cuddly.
And if he acts up, you can knock
the stuffing out of him.)

The Perfect Man.

(He's young. He's cute.
And no matter where you go, he
can't keep his eyes off you.)

The Perfect Man.

(He's rich. He's strong.
And he's actually capable
of feeding himself.)

The Perfect Man.

(He's cute. He's entertaining.
And he always
lets you be in control.)

The Perfect Man.

(He's quiet. He's sweet. And if he gives you any grief, you can bite his head off.)

The Perfect Man.

(He's young. He's cute.
And he always comes crawling
back to you.)

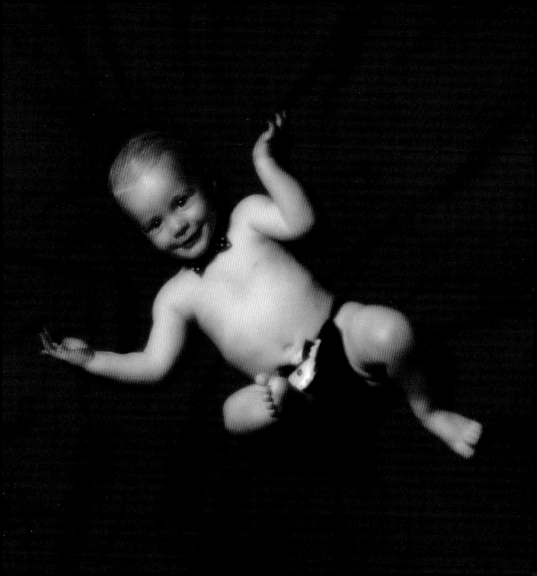

The Perfect Man.

(He's quiet. He's easily amused. And you'll always know exactly where to find him.)

The Perfect Man.

(He's strong. He's tough. And he actually likes it when you order him around.)

The
Perfect
Man.

(He's handsome. He's talented.
And he'll always
be rolling in the dough.)

The Perfect Man.

(He's romantic. He's cute. And he has ten zillion frequent flyer miles.)

The Perfect Man.

(He's nice. He's happy.
And no matter what you say,
he'll nod in agreement.)

The Perfect Man.

(He's sweet. He's simple. And he'll actually believe everything you tell him.)

The Perfect Man.

(He's cute. He's talented.
And you'll always know who wears
the pants in the family.)

The Perfect Man.

(He's quiet. He's mysterious.
And if he ever lies to you,
you can see right through him.)

The Perfect Man.

(He's tall. He's thin.
And if a cuter guy calls, you
can just leave him hanging.)

The Perfect Man.

(He's sweet. He's rich.
And he knows what it takes
to really satisfy a woman.)

The Perfect Man.

(He's smooth. He's well-rounded.
And if he looks at another girl,
just crack him one.)

The Perfect Man.

(He's attractive. He's funny.
And if he loses his hair,
you just put it back on.)

The Perfect Man.

(He's romantic. He's noble.
And he's the perfect guy for
a one-knight-stand.)

The Perfect Man.

(He cooks. He cleans.
And the more you eat,
the better he likes you.)

The Perfect Man.

(He's quiet. He's helpful. And only half of what comes out of his mouth is nuts.)

The Perfect Man.

(He can't talk about sports.
He can't talk about cars. And best of all,
he can't talk about himself.)

The Perfect Man.

(He's cute. He's handy.
And you've always got him wrapped
around your finger.)

The Perfect Man.

(He's cute. He's playful.
And if he gives you any trouble,
you can ring his neck.)

The Perfect Man.

(He's intelligent. He's sophisticated. And he's really easy to turn on.)

The
Perfect
Man.

(He's nice. He's funny.
And, best of all, it's really easy
to push him around.)

The Perfect Man.

(He's happy. He's fun.
And you can always make him bend
over backward for you.)

The Perfect Man.

(He's quiet. He's exotic.
And he almost always
gets your point.)

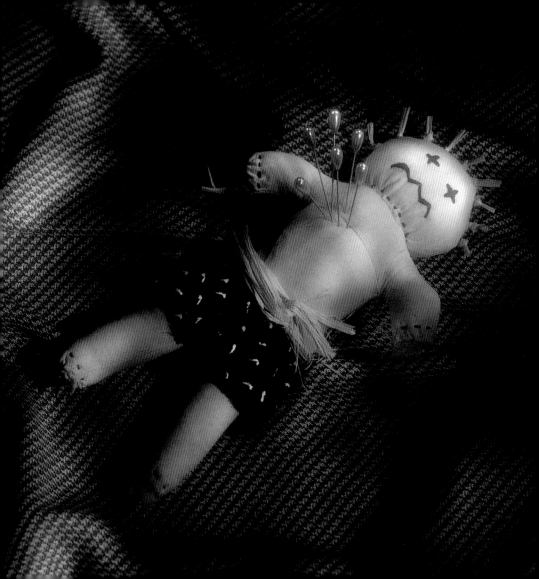

The Perfect Man.

(He's funny. He's flexible.
And you've always got him right
in the palm of your hand.)

The
Perfect
Man.

(He's funny. He's entertaining.
And, unlike most guys,
he actually has rhythm.)

The Perfect Man.

(He's cool. He's well-rounded. And he actually knows how to use a broom.)

The Perfect Man.

(He's sweet. He's loaded.
And after a bad day, you can
twist his head off.)

The Perfect Man.

(He never snores. Or burps.
And if he does, just
knock the wind out of him.)

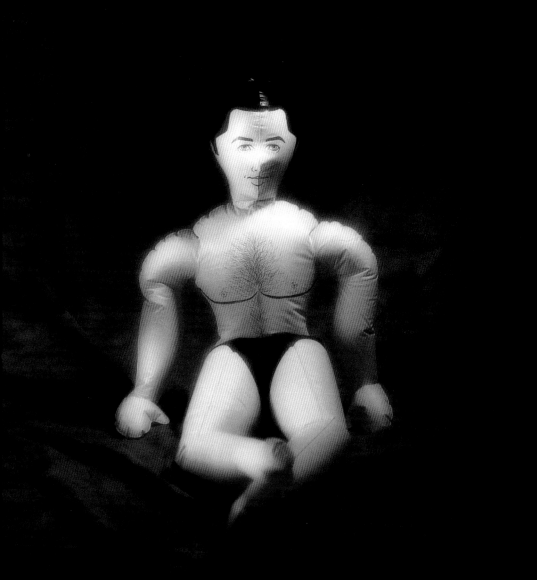

The Perfect Man.

(He's thoughtful. He's kind. And if you rub his belly, you'll always get lucky.)

The Perfect Man.

(He's bright. He's warm.
And he can actually
stay hot all night.)

The Perfect Man.

(He cooks. He cleans.
And if you ever get bored, you can
put him on the back burner.)

The Perfect Man.

(He's tall. He's handsome.
And if he talks back, just get out
the weed whacker.)

The Perfect Man.

(He's cute. He's flexible.
And he's always willing to
let you do the talking.)

The Perfect Man.

(He's sweet. He's open.
And he's always more than willing
to spill his guts.)

The Perfect Man.

(He's cute. He's quiet.
And he only opens his mouth
when you want him to.)

The Perfect Man.

(He's cute. He's funny.
And he never leaves
the seat up.)

©2003 Debra White Smith

ISBN 1-58660-728-6

Senior Editor: Rebecca Germany
Editorial Consultant: Susan Downs
Layout designer: Anita Cook

Published by Promise Press, an imprint of Barbour Publishing, Inc., P.O. Box 719, Uhrichsville, Ohio 44683, www.promisepress.com

Member of the
Evangelical Christian
Publishers Association

Printed in the United States of America.
5 4 3 2 1

The

Key

A N°VELLA

DEBRA WHITE SMITH

PROMISE PRESS

An Imprint of Barbour Publishing

Dedicated to my all-time favorite locksmith,
my husband, Daniel Smith.

Chapter One

$\mathcal{B}$rendy Lane gaped at Ezekiel Blake. Zeke, her high school sweetheart. Her first love. The man for whom she had promised to wait when he went off to Vietnam some thirty-three years ago. The man she had jilted for Mack.

Her cheeks flashed hot, and then chilled just as quickly as they'd heated. She gripped her coffee shop's counter and swallowed an exclamation. Her father had always attributed her spontaneous tongue to the presence of her fiery locks. Problem was, her natural hair color had been a long way from fiery for several years. Nevertheless, her former fiancé's presence evoked a storm of emotions that would have produced a barrage of

5

nervous babbling if she were still in her youth. Instead, Brendy left all babbling to the mockingbird, whose song floated from the oak near the open door.

"Ziggy!" She croaked the old endearment as if she had seen a ghost from the halls of Jacksonville High School.

The year had been 1970, and they'd been voted the senior class sweetheart and beau. By the time the two walked across the stage for their award, the boys' basketball team was chanting, "Ziggy. . . Ziggy. . .Ziggy."

"Hi, Brendy." Zeke tilted his head to one side, and the morning sun highlighted silver threads in his thick, black hair. A smile, tentative yet teasing, increased the lines around one of his eyes. A white patch covered the other, and Brendy stopped herself short of asking what happened to his eye. She hadn't seen him since that teary moment she waved as the Greyhound bus whisked him out of Jacksonville, heading for boot camp. In her youthful sorrow, she dreaded the thought that he might land in the Vietnamese jungle. Minutes before his departure she pledged her undying faithfulness. . .no matter what.

"Mom mentioned you'd opened a new coffee and gift shop." Zeke hooked a thumb in his jeans belt loop and scanned the shelves, lined with specialty coffees and a wide array of country gifts. "I wondered when you called if it was you."

"C–called?" she questioned and wrinkled her brow. An overstuffed, striped feline rubbed against her legs, and Tiger-Higer produced a pitiful meow that sounded like a high-pitched echo of Brendy's word.

"Yes—for a locksmith," Zeke answered. He rested his weight on his left leg in a gesture that suggested he was settling in for a long conversation.

"Oh! A locksmith!" Brendy blurted. "Yes—I–I—you mean that would be you?"

"Yes, that would be me." His deep voice floated around the quaint store like liquid satin, and Brendy shivered against a delightful chill that danced up her spine. She had heard through the grapevine that Zeke was back in town. She'd even picked up the news that he opened a locksmith business. But that information hadn't crossed her mind when she snatched the phone book and dialed the first locksmith who was listed—B and B Locksmith Service.

"Well, uh, th–thanks for coming so—so s–soon." Brendy released the counter and began stroking her over-sized apron. The smells of gourmet coffee and chocolates mingled with the scent of the vanilla candles she'd just placed near the cash register. Brendy sucked in a deep breath and reveled in the sudden rush of expectation that assaulted her from nowhere. All at once, she wondered if the smell of vanilla would forever remind her of the day Ezekiel Blake stepped back into her life.

"So, this is your little place?" Zeke asked. He closed the door, and the bell merrily clanged against the glass panes of the door.

"Yes, this is 'The Friend-Shop'!" She awkwardly waved her hand to encompass the quaint home-turned-shop that represented a six-year dream to own her own business. The polished hardwood floors and knotty-pine walls served as a perfect backdrop for the 1950s-style coffee bar where Brendy served hot coffee and home-made cookies.

Presently, a klatch of four retired locals sat in the corner, sipping their coffee and playing checkers. But the main thing they usually accomplished was gossiping about the "latest" around the sleepy town of Jacksonville, Texas—where, for the past fifty years, time had seemingly stood still. One of those checkers warriors looked up from a time-intensive move, slipped his narrow reading glasses down his nose, and eyed Zeke as if he were the latest piece of juicy news. Indeed, Mr. Narvy's three checkers partners followed their *compadre*'s lead, and all paused to examine Zeke.

Brendy's stomach did flip-flops, and warmth oozed from her midsection into her limbs. When the checkers brigade shifted their focus from Zeke to Brendy, she resisted the urge to shrink to her knees and hide behind the counter. Brendy wondered how long it would take for this meeting between her and Zeke to spread along the social grapevine. Brendy had long ago ended the hallucination that she could ever keep secrets in a town with a population just over thirteen thousand. She figured the seniors' Sunday school class would be abuzz with all manner of conjectures, and that was exactly forty-eight hours away.

"So. . ." The hardwood floor creaked as Zeke neared.

Brendy snapped her attention back to him. Yet all she could think of was their first kiss—which was Brendy's *very first* kiss.

At the age of sixteen, she and Zeke went on a picnic with her parents. The summer sun glistened across Lake Jacksonville like a shower of glitter. Zeke asked Brendy's dad for permission to take a walk around the lake, and she despaired that her father would say no. When he agreed, the sun shone a little brighter, the breeze seemed a bit more refreshing, the birds sang just for Zeke and Brendy. When Brendy first noticed the weeping willow, the summer wind whispered through its limbs and summoned them closer. Zeke tugged her trembling hand, and the two of them walked toward the willow. She hoped

Zeke might kiss her there. Oh, how she hoped. Soon they paused under the weeping willow. . . .

"You said you were having trouble with a lock?"

Zeke's words seemed to float across the lake upon a balmy zephyr that lifted her hair and christened her cheeks. Brendy started and blinked. "Uh. . .a–a lock. Yes—yes, I have a lock. I mean, I have a *problem* with a lock." Her knees wobbled as fiercely as they had years ago when Zeke's lips brushed hers in a chaste caress that tilted her world. "It's—it's the back—the back lock," she said on a snatch of breath.

Zeke rubbed slender fingers along the edge of the bandage that covered one eye, and a tender smile revealed the twin dimples she had adored as a teenager. She held his gaze a fraction longer than the checkers brigade would claim was decent. Then she looked a little deeper into his soul, and Brendy would have pledged that she saw the weeping willow. . .the lake. . . and the undying flames of first love.

Get a grip! she admonished herself. *You're a woman over fifty. You aren't a teenager, and neither is Ziggy. He's probably married anyway!*

Brendy couldn't stop herself from glancing at his left hand, where no gold band claimed his ring finger. Her pulse pounded at the base of her throat, and she touched the inside of her own wedding band. The wedding band she had refused to stop wearing even after ten years as a widow. Her pledge of loyalty to the memory of her children's father had been the force behind the continued presence of the wedding ring.

But in the face of Zeke's warm appraisal, Brendy realized with aching poignancy that loyalty to a memory did little to keep her warm at night.

Tiger-Higer plopped his striped self atop the counter and stuck his nose squarely into the midst of the vanilla candles. "No, no," Brendy admonished. "It's time for you to go out anyway." She grabbed her grandchildren's pet and clung to him as the most logical diversion available. *And, heaven help me, I need a diversion,* she thought. *The checkers brigade is going to have enough fodder for the gossip chain for months if I don't cool it!*

"Come on back, Zeke," Brendy called over her shoulder and applauded her ability to finally sound as if she were getting down to business. "The lock with the problem is back here."

Zeke followed Brendy behind the counter. As he neared the doorway to the other rooms, the skin along his spine crawled with the sensation of being watched. Zeke darted a glance toward that checkers gang. As if they were one, the knot of men simultaneously shifted their attention to the checkerboard. With a shake of his head, Zeke followed Brendy past an office and into a storage room that opened to the backyard. Along the hallway, he stepped around a Barbie cash register and a Hot Wheels race car set. *Must be grandchildren,* he thought, yet the observation served as a spear to his heart. Undoubtedly when Brendy jilted him to marry Mack Lane, she found the man of her dreams. *They're probably still dreaming together.* He couldn't stop the twist of unexpected jealousy that shot through his belly. Even after his own marriage and raising his children—even after all these years—he couldn't deny he'd never completely gotten over his first love.

As they paused beside the door and Brendy tossed out the striped tomcat, the familiar scent of Shalimar overshadowed the smell of cappuccino. He had introduced Brendy to the fragrance the Christmas of their senior year.

The aroma now evoked memories of those carefree days. A time before war and loss. A time when they nearly married, yet separated forever. A time that seemed so close, yet so far away.

Brendy inserted her hand into the pocket of a

butcher's apron that covered most of her slacks and hand-painted T-shirt.

Thirty-three years ago, at Lake Jacksonville, Brendy held out a supple hand. Zeke then slid his senior ring on its fourth finger. The smooth skin yielded as the sign of his pledge slipped into place.

They had attended the athletic banquet at school, and a clutch of couples drifted out to Lake Jacksonville. Young love filled the sweet autumn night. The pairs scattered, leaving Zeke free to extend his ring to Brendy. Then, holding hands, they walked toward their favorite spot. A weeping willow grew beside three large iron-ore rocks at the edge of the lake. The rising moon shed circles of light upon the rippling water like bands of glowing satin strung by fairies of the deep. The two exchanged no words. None were necessary. The gentle pressure of her hand told him volumes.

They stopped. She turned. He answered by a caress of her cheek. Zeke tilted her chin upward until their lips met. The delicate kiss lasted only a moment but was filled with an eternity of commitment as his ring glistened in the moon's luminescence.

Now, her hands were showing wear, and there was a

band of gold where Zeke's ring had been.

"When I arrived this morning, the key opened the lock, as usual, but it froze up and I can't even get the key to come out now." Brendy bent over the ornery lock, and her fingers flitted around it.

Her honey-toned voice woke Zeke from his reverie. More than anything he longed to say, "I've still got the key to your heart." He dared not. The wedding band meant she still belonged to Mack Lane.

The shop's bell rang. She rose and looked back the way they had come. "Oh, rats," she whispered, then her face crumpled into a smile that seemed to light up the whole musty hallway. The smile Zeke would never forget. The smile that had implanted itself upon his heart and refused to release him.

"Would you believe it?" she asked and shook her head. Her copper curls danced delightfully around her cheeks. "I've been praying for more business, and now that it's here, I'm saying 'rats.' "

Zeke rested a hand on the doorknob and leaned into his good leg. "Look," he said, "go on and take care of your business. I'll see to this problem. As soon as I figure out what you need to do, I'll meander back up front."

"Okay." Brendy's eyes, as green as the finest Vietnamese jade, turned toward him, and she seemed ready to hang onto his every word. Zeke wasn't prepared for the longing stirring her soul. Longing—and a hint of remorse. He stopped himself from taking in a hissing breath and felt as if the tidal wave of attraction would take him under. If Zeke didn't know any better, he'd say he was eighteen again.

She tried to step past him in the narrow hall. Yet their attempts to keep from bumping into each other resulted in the two of them doing something akin to the jitterbug. Indeed, by the time she was sashaying up the hallway, Zeke's pulse *was* doing the jitterbug.

But she's married! he reminded himself and stared at the gold band on her ring finger until she disappeared into the store.

Zeke purposefully stepped from the shop and into the bright morning sunshine, hoping to remove himself from the magnetic pull of the woman within. Yet a lattice full of honeysuckle hugged the back of the house and reminded him of their senior prom. Someone had thought it clever to lay branches of fresh honeysuckle along the center of the round tables. Brendy loved the idea and had even tucked a strand behind her ear.

As a cool spring breeze danced through the pines, oaks, and maples, Zeke scowled at the honeysuckle. *I need to get out of here,* he decided. *As in, move back to*

Houston while I still have some pride left. A squirrel's scoffing bark seemed a response to his thoughts. Zeke glanced over his shoulder and into the inky gaze of a gray squirrel who protested his interruption.

"I hear ya. I hear ya. I'm not after your babies," he responded and purposed to focus upon the task at hand. After examining the doorknob, Zeke pronounced the thing worn out—irrevocably and completely. He eyed the repaired eaves of the home-turned-store and figured the lock was the original. "The thing is probably seventy years old," he diagnosed.

Zeke stepped back into the hallway and peered toward the store. In the distance, Brendy chatted with a lady who deliberated over two candles. For a flash, he was tempted to just go around the store, get a new knob out of his van, fix it, and mail Brendy a bill. While that route seemed the safest and most sane, Zeke knew he couldn't compromise his usual business procedures. He *never* made a change unless his customers approved and understood the cost. The only way Brendy could approve his diagnosis would be if he discussed the problem with her.

He scraped together all his courage and ambled up the hallway, doing his best to hide his slight limp. Zeke hadn't felt self-conscious about his missing leg in years. Being near Brendy somehow reawakened those first feelings of inadequacy after the terrible battle that also took his eye. He touched the patch the doctor had placed on yesterday. "Wear this a day or two and keep the socket clean. Make sure you use this antibiotic ointment three times a day. I know this is irritating, but it's a simple infection. Your socket should be cleared up in a day or two and you can put your prosthesis back in." Zeke had agreed and gladly followed the doctor's instructions.

He wondered if it would make any difference to Brendy that he had not only lost a leg in the jungles of Vietnam but an eye as well. He stroked the thin scar that coursed the edge of his right jaw. The horror of the firefight at Phong Din—a little-known but deadly battle— traced its way through his memory.

When he regained consciousness three days after the battle, his eye and leg were gone, and a row of neat stitches dotted his jaw.

Zeke stepped into the store as Brendy finalized the sale. She graciously smiled at the snowy-haired lady and even threw in a sample bag of French vanilla coffee. Zeke had longed for that smile during those months of convalescence. Looking back, he wondered if thoughts of Brendy were what kept him alive.

Buckets full of morning sun spilled through the line of windows along the east wall and illuminated the locks of Brendy's auburn hair. In another life, she had caught the wavy locks into a bouncy ponytail that swayed with her every step. Now the fiery ringlets hugged her ears and neckline in a full, easy-swing style that suited her just as much as the ponytail. She'd kept her figure nicely as well. Her shoulders sloped a bit and her waist didn't pinch at the middle quite like it had at age eighteen. Still, as Zeke matured, he preferred a woman with some meat on her bones anyway.

Brendy bade her customer farewell, and the aging lady with spry blue eyes looked Zeke up and down. "You Ezekiel Blake?" she asked.

"Yes," he answered. "Yes, I am." The angle of the lady's arched brows and firm jaw struck him as familiar, yet he couldn't place her. Zeke rested a hand on the rustic counter and leaned off his prosthesis.

"Eloise Thom," the lady said and tugged on her lavender sweater as if she were the authority at large. "When you were a freshman, I sent you to the principal's office for pulling a girl's ponytail," she said as if the very memory made her want to repeat the punishment.

"Oh, Mrs. Thom," Zeke said and extended a hand to his former English teacher. "Yes, I *knew* you looked familiar."

She clasped his hand and winked. "I believe the girl

with the ponytail was *she,* if I'm not mistaken." Mrs. Thom nodded toward Brendy.

Zeke chuckled. "Yes, I believe you are right." He stole a glimpse at Brendy, whose cheeks now matched her hair. She busied herself with a pile of receipts that crackled with the activity. A cursory glance toward the checkers brigade revealed they were processing more information for later discussion.

"I was so sorry to hear of your dear wife's death, Ezekiel," Mrs. Thom said, and Zeke was almost certain she was projecting her voice over the sound of the rattling receipts.

"Well, that was five years ago," Zeke supplied.

"Hmm, and I guess Brendy's dear husband had been gone a good five years before that." She shook her head and turned toward the door. "It's all a crying shame."

Zeke dashed a glance to Brendy's ring finger, and his attention was drawn to her candid eyes. She didn't look away. No, indeed. Brendy Lane tentatively held his gaze. Without a word, she confirmed Mrs. Thom's statement.

"Toodles," Mrs. Thom called before reaching the door. Zeke would have sworn in court that the old lady sent an exaggerated wink to the checkers guards.

Brendy made a monumental task of counting those crinkled receipts again. At the rate she was going, Zeke calculated the things would disintegrate. The doorbell jingled, Mrs. Thom stepped outside, and Brendy called after her, "Thank you, Mrs. Thom. Come back."

"Come back. . .come back. . .come back." Her words reverberated from the past and tore at his heart.

The month after graduation, the draft board sent Zeke a notice. College and a deferment were the best choice, but he needed the money the army offered. Imagining himself a mighty warrior, Zeke stepped up to his responsibility to serve his country.

Brendy cried when he told her about the army. Even his arms failed to hush her weeping. "Promise me you'll come back," she begged. And between sobs, she pledged to be waiting when he returned. His heavy class ring upon her finger pressed into the back of Zeke's neck as if she were trying to keep him from the dreaded departure. She kissed him until desperation blended into heartache. Each kiss evidenced her vow. All so long ago.

Boot camp was a blur, yet Zeke would never forget the sight of South Vietnam as they descended toward their battleground. He recalled those initial days, frenzied and full of overwrought nerves, wondering if he'd been crazy to imagine himself as a military hero. Bemoaning the agony of living without his Brendy. Only her letters kept Zeke sane. He remembered standing in mud or drizzle or blinding sun as Sergeant Myles called the names of those getting mail. The mere mention of his name always assured Zeke he could make it another day. The letters did come every day for a season. Then they dwindled: three per week, four a month, once every six weeks, and then finally, none. Several of his buddies experienced the same, and they silently bore each other up while pretending they didn't care. Deep inside, the despair almost crushed Zeke.

Now, with her closeness palpable, all the plans and hopes of those lost days rushed upon Zeke. The fragments of dreams fell at his feet. He stood close enough to touch the woman he once yearned to marry. Now, years later, they had both loved. . .and lost.

And Zeke wondered if Brendy Lane remembered. Did she remember the weeping willow. . .the moon's satin ribbons on Lake Jacksonville. . .the honeysuckle. . .the promise of eternal love? Or was it all dashed aside the minute she met Mack Lane?

"I'm going to need to replace your lock," he said and was amazed at the calm timbre of his voice.

"Y–yes. Yes, of course." As she rearranged the cookies in the glass display case, a lock of her copper hair grazed the apple of her cheek—a cheek his lips had brushed. Zeke rubbed his callused thumb against his fingers and wondered if her skin was as soft as when she was eighteen. The faint hint of Shalimar beckoned him to caress her face, and Zeke decided this was a locksmith job he was doing for free.

Chapter Two

*B*rendy could barely perform her routine duties with Zeke working in the back. She felt as if some force from the past beckoned her to his side, tugged her to his heart, demanded they rediscover the love of youth—so tender, yet so fierce. Nevertheless, Brendy resisted the urge to watch Zeke work. She resisted so hard and with such determination that she didn't even know Zeke had gone until her part-time employee, Sylvia Donnelley, scooted through the front door at ten A.M.

"Is that a locksmith pulling out of our drive?" Sylvia asked, her blond curls swinging around her face. Sylvia's pudgy legs and round face attested to the pralines she snitched from the glass-front display. Even so, the young woman possessed the most exotic pair of sea green eyes Brendy had ever encountered.

"Uh, yes, that's a locksmith," Brendy admitted. She aimed her bottle of glass cleaner and sprayed an imaginary bit of dust on a display case filled with gourmet chocolate. As she swiped away the cleaner, she suspected this was the third time she'd gone over this shelf in the last half hour.

Only when one of the checkers crew cleared his throat did Brendy realize Sylvia said the locksmith van was *leaving*. Feigning a casual yawn, Brendy stepped to the window and pretended to wipe at a smudge. Instead, she strained to see Zeke's gray van troll past the brick library and turn the corner beside McDonald's.

He didn't leave a bill, she thought. *Or say good-bye.* The latter realization sent a stab of regret through her.

By the time Brendy turned back around, she witnessed Sylvia, coffeepot in hand, leaning close to Mr. Narvy. The gnarled gentleman's right brow rose, and his bushy gray mustache twittered around his words as if he were sharing a CIA secret.

Sylvia's wide-eyed nod was accompanied by a stolen glance toward Brendy. When she encountered her boss's stare, Sylvia ducked her head and busied herself refilling coffee cups.

Wasting no time, Brendy deposited her dust cloth and Windex on the counter, trod down the hallway, and straight to the back door. A shiny new lock now gleamed against the freshly painted door. A sparkling set of keys hung from a slither of tape in the center of the door; beside the keys was a note in a distinctive script she had never forgotten.

Brendy,
　　This one's on me. Call if you need me again. You have my number. And, by the way, you look great! The years have been good to you.
　　　　　　　　　　　　　　　　Yours, Ziggy

Brendy snared the note and keys from the door and leaned against the wall. She read and reread the note half a dozen times before she closed her eyes and allowed herself to admit the truth. *I never got over him.* The admission opened a river of love that spilled through her being in warm witness of two hearts that were never fully able to express their undying devotion.

Brendy had never planned to jilt Zeke. Indeed, the day she watched the Greyhound bus whisk away her love she would have gone to her grave vowing her heart would

25

forever be true. But Brendy had only been eighteen. *Eighteen.* As the days blended to weeks and the weeks to months, she began to taste loneliness on a most desperate level.

When Mack Lane entered the church that fine September Sunday, Brendy hadn't stopped herself from taking a second, third, and fourth look. His blond hair, mysterious brown eyes, and finely chiseled features sent the whole row of teenage girls into gaping fits. The grapevine was alive and well as always. Word had it that Mack Lane was the nephew of their pastor and had come to live with him while attending Lon Morris College.

By the time Brendy sneaked a fifth look at the newcomer, she realized he was looking back at *her*. So she took a sixth look! Despite the presence of Zeke's senior ring evoking a cloud of guilt, Brendy strategically placed herself by the back door after service. She simply didn't bother to shy away when Mack paused to chat.

The rest was history. A whirlwind courtship. Married by spring. Their first child a year later. And somewhere in the middle of it all, Brendy tucked her promise to Zeke in a corner of her soul. She told herself he'd find someone new, just like she had, and that he'd be as happy as she. Despite her rationale, Brendy never shook the nagging sense that she would have walked down the aisle for Zeke if he hadn't been drafted.

Brendy dared read the note again, and tears welled in her eyes. Tears that refused suppression. She stepped back up the hallway and called to Sylvia, "I'm going to be in my office awhile," and didn't deny that her voice sounded strained. She could only imagine what the checkers brigade must be thinking.

She moved into the office that looked like a tornado had struck. Along with a pile of papers covering the desk, an overflowing toy box claimed one corner. Her grand-children's art projects decorated the opposite wall, and an array of their playclothes had been scattered near the closet. When their mother abandoned the children and Brendy's son two years ago, Brendy found herself filling the role of mother once more. Her son Kent moved back home with his children, and they all struggled together the best they could. As always, Brendy wondered if that vixen of a mother of theirs, way out in California ever thought of them. She clenched her teeth and suppressed the bitter bile welling from her soul. Never had Brendy so struggled with the temptation to retaliate against an-other person.

Yet today another broken relationship demanded presidence in her thoughts—a relationship *she* had ended.

Brendy scrubbed the back of her hand against a tear trickling down her cheek and picked a path through the clutter. She settled into her leather chair, laid Zeke's note on the desk, and covered her face with her hands. The smell of Shalimar perfume filled her senses.

The year was 1969. The Christmas Eve spirit hugged her parent's frame home like a cozy blanket. The trees, barren and gray, strained against the cold breeze. The misty clouds predicted the coming of a long-anticipated white Christmas, a rare treat in east Texas. Zeke arrived promptly at ten of five and bustled Brendy into the black Mustang his parents helped him buy. The two lovebirds didn't really have anyplace to go, and the small town of Jacksonville certainly didn't offer a wide array of choices.

So Zeke drove out to Love's Lookout, a scenic roadside park that overlooked the east Texas rolling hills and provided a breathtaking view of Lookout Valley. The two bundled up and walked hand in hand near the rock wall, poised on a precipice that descended straight into clumps of pines. Brendy and Zeke paused and absorbed the miles and miles of trees and hills as well as the occasional peek at homes nestled amidst the woods. The crisp winter breeze smelled of evergreens, and Brendy imagined that, if Zeke ever got around to proposing, they would be in their own home, with their own Christmas tree, by this time next year.

Zeke's cleared his throat and dug his hand into his coat pocket. He pulled out a tiny red box, too big for a ring, but too little for anything Brendy could imagine. The green velvet bow shivered in the breeze, and Brendy leaned into Zeke as he spoke his heart. "I couldn't wait a minute longer," he said. "I. . .hope you like it."

She gazed up into his vulnerable blue eyes and reverently took the package. Looking back, Brendy understood now that, somewhere along the way, Ezekiel Blake had irrevocably lost his heart—lost it to her.

Brendy wasted no time in unwrapping the package. In her haste, the paper and ribbon fell to their feet; and Brendy was left holding a box of perfume—*real perfume!* Breathless, she had thrown herself into his arms, and the two rocked as she squealed with glee. Zeke's pulled away and bestowed a gentle kiss upon her waiting lips. He helped her remove the cellophane from the box and dabble just a touch of the perfume upon her wrists and behind her ears.

That evening, Brendy declared Shalimar her favorite perfume, and a scattering of tiny snowflakes falling like white diamonds seemed to christen the moment.

The day she met Mack, Brendy stopped wearing the

cherished fragrance. She didn't start wearing it again until a year after her husband's heart attack and subsequent death. Brendy stumbled across the cherished bottle tucked in a keepsake box at the back of her closet. Surprisingly, the fragrance was still sweet. After she'd used the rest of it, Brendy placed the empty bottle back into the box and bought herself more Shalimar. She'd been loyal to the scent ever since. Deep inside she wondered if, perhaps, she'd worn the fragrance in the hopes that Zeke might one day return and understand she never forgot him. Such whimsical notions had seemed far-fetched—until today.

Brendy lifted her face from her hands, now damp with the essence of her poignant reverie. She pulled open her oak desk's bottom drawer, dropped to her knees, and reached beneath the clutter to the back. Her fingers encountered a small padded box, covered in satin, once royal blue, now nearly gray; topped with a rose, once peachy, now pale. She shoved aside a mound of paperwork on her desktop. As if she were handling the rarest of treasures, Brendy settled the oval box upon the desk, lifted the lid, and absorbed the essence of the treasures within. The empty perfume bottle. A dried corsage from the prom. A senior ring, swathed in tape. A yellowed photo of Zeke in his letter jacket. And underneath it all, a golden locket, strangely lacking tarnish. Zeke had presented her with the locket on Valentine's Day of their junior year. They placed a photo of themselves inside, and Zeke kept the key while Brendy wore the locket.

Now, Brendy pressed the locket to her lips and wondered if Zeke still had the key. Before she had the chance to analyze her motives, she clasped the necklace around her neck and tucked the heart beneath her decorative T-shirt.

A shaft of morning sun pierced the windows and glimmered against her gold wedding band. Brendy eyed the symbol of her vow and pondered her deceased husband. Mack had been good to her. Really good. He adored her and lavished her with the love, loyalty, and respect many women crave their whole lives but die never knowing. Brendy had been devastated when the call came that he was the victim of a massive heart attack. He'd been dead upon arrival at the hospital, at the age of forty-one. All these years Brendy wore the band as a symbol of loyalty to the man whose son and daughter she bore. The golden band twinkled up at her as if to say its purpose had been fulfilled. *Mack would want me to be happy*, she thought. With a sense of deep peace, she twisted the gold band off her finger and examined the tan line left behind. Before she could change her mind, Brendy dropped the ring into the padded box.

"Oh, Lord," she breathed, "Mack always said You work in mysterious ways. I'm mystified, to say the least. Guide my steps. I don't want to make any mistakes. But You know there's always been a place in my heart for Ziggy, and if I'm not badly mistaken, he feels the same."

Zeke Blake parked his van by the duplex he rented from Major Purvis on Cherry Street. His landlord imagined himself a big man around Jacksonville. He wasn't a big man in any sense of the word. His parents gave him the name *Major*, not the military. The only distinction Major carried was being the owner of more junk property than anyone in town. Zeke found him a good man to do business with, so Zeke handled all the security problems of Purvis's rental property. They had struck a work-for-rent agreement, and since the amount of work was moderate, Zeke considered the deal advantageous. His plan included banking his disability payments and supporting himself with the income of his locksmith business. When he added all this to the equity received on the home he had sold, the sum was tidy.

Moving back to the town of his birth had been a necessity to help care for his aging mother, who lived only two streets over. During the last nine months, he'd become involved in his small community church. But in a town the size of Jacksonville, most single groups were tailored to college-aged people. Therefore, the downside of his move proved to be loneliness.

Zeke checked his watch. He'd been out answering calls most of the day, and now three-thirty steadily approached. He secured the lock on his van, which housed thousands of dollars in equipment. After limping toward the aging duplex, he unlocked the door and shuffled into the frame home, filled with his deceased wife's country decor. Yet this afternoon his thoughts weren't with the woman who nursed him through his physical recovery. Instead, they were with the woman who broke his heart.

Nostalgia was taking him under. With purpose in his step, Zeke strode through the house toward the spare bedroom. He rummaged under the heavy four-poster bed until his worn hands rested upon the box, taped tight for years. He tugged the box across the short-piled carpet the color of plums, then reached for his pocket-knife. Zeke wasted no time slitting the tape and gazing upon the musty contents. He'd told himself when he found the dust-laden box in his mother's garage that he was a sentimental old fool for hanging onto it. Nevertheless, he couldn't allow himself to discard a single item within.

Zeke dug past high school annuals, a few chipped trophies, and a basketball jersey. At the bottom of it all rested a scratched-up cardboard box the size of a business card. Zeke opened the box and pulled out a tarnished key attached to a short chain long enough to wrap around a couple of his fingers. He held up the key and watched it dangle in the afternoon light as if dancing with glee to be out of the box.

Zeke pressed the keepsake against his palm. As he closed his fingers around it, more memories he'd thought long forgotten bombarded him. But most of all, the words he and Brendy pledged reverberated through the corridors of his lonely heart. *Undying love. Always for each other. Nothing can come between us.* A hundred worn-out clichés that never came true.

His cell phone emitted the beginning of "America the Beautiful" from his belt. Zeke rocked back on his heels and sighed. Today was Friday. The weekends were usually the busiest days for a locksmith. He and his jovial mother usually joked that people weren't any good on their own. Once they started getting off work for the weekend, they began locking themselves out of their cars and homes.

He stood, kicked the box back under the bed, and retrieved his cell. Still clutching the key, he pressed the *answer* button and spoke the usual greeting. This time, the words sounded less than enthusiastic.

"Uh, Ziggy?" Brendy's hesitant voice sounded over the line, and the tarnished key seemed to warm in his grasp.

"Yes?" he rasped. Was his voice cracking like a fourteen year old or was he imagining things?

"I. . .uh. . .you said in your note to call you if I needed you again."

She needs me! he thought. *Yes!*

"Of course," he responded. "Is there another problem with your lock?" *I love you,* he thought. *I never stopped, you know.* "I meant to tell you in the note that I placed the old one on the back steps."

"No. It has nothing to do with *that* lock," she said on a sheepish note. "I'm here at Jacksonville Christian School." The sound of a child's high-pitched squeal attested to her claim. "You two stop it now!" she admonished. "Sorry, Zeke, I wasn't talking to you."

He chuckled and gazed out the room's window toward a circle of dwarf crepe myrtles in his backyard.

"It's my grandchildren. I'm helping raise them. They're trying to wrestle each other to the floor right here in the principal's office," she continued in a harassed voice. "Listen, I've locked my keys in my car. Would you please come—?"

"I'll be there in five minutes," he agreed and acknowledged the location and color of her Chevy minivan.

As Zeke disconnected the call, he was tempted to leap out back, snatch a handful of crepe myrtle blooms, and present them to Brendy after he unlocked her car. Instead, he decided to behave like a fifty-one-year-old man instead of an adolescent. So he dropped the old key into his shirt pocket, fastened the button at the top, and marched off to rescue the woman who'd been his high school sweetheart. His leading lady. The woman who was now his damsel in distress.

$\mathcal{H}$ere he comes," Brendy sighed as Zeke's gray Chevy van pulled into the parking lot of Jacksonville Christian School. He gassed his vehicle into the drive that circled through the parking lot and headed straight for her van. Her straw-headed, blue-eyed grandchildren jumped up from the short brick wall under the portico and dashed toward the driveway just as Zeke's van drew parallel with them.

Brakes screeched.

Gravel flew.

And Brendy screamed, "Stop!"

The children halted. Pete glared at the locksmith while Pat hovered close beside him.

"You two almost got run over!" Brendy scolded and covered her heart with her trembling hand. "You know better than to run out into this driveway."

"He should have been watching better," Pete retorted and marched toward Brendy's cobalt blue minivan. Her head hung, Pat followed in his wake.

"Pete," Brendy threatened, "watch your attitude, young man."

He shot her a glare, and Brendy wavered between gathering him in her arms and sentencing him to time-out when they got to the store. Filling the shoes of their mother kept Brendy in a constant state of upheaval. They were hurting, and there wasn't a thing she could do to erase their past.

Indeed, that very day Brendy had been summoned to a teacher's meeting. There, she had been informed that Pete was continuing to disrupt his second grade class. On top of that, he started a fight that day during recess. Pat was a different story. Now in all-day kindergarten, the child seemed to be recessing deeper and deeper into a shell. Her teacher was looking for ways to encourage Pat to speak up more.

At last, her grandmother's heart won. With a sigh, Brendy moved between the children and placed an arm around each of them. She figured Pete had been through enough discipline today without her heaping more on him.

This morning, the May sunshine had tenderly caressed the countryside, but an unseasonable warm spell caused the temperature to hit ninety. Now the beads of perspiration upon the children's upper lips matched the moisture along Brendy's neckline. *I'd probably be grouchy too,* she thought, *if I was only eight and hot as a pistol.*

Zeke's van crunched to a stop beside hers. When his door slammed, Brendy recalled the locket still around her neck. She fumbled with the chain and made certain the heart rested beneath her painted T-shirt. The second she was confident of the locket's covering, Zeke rounded his van wearing a smile the size of Texas. The lines around his eyes crinkled, and that lone patch over his eye nearly prompted Brendy once again to inquire about his problem. Nevertheless, she refrained. *Probably just an irritation or something,* she mused. In his hand Zeke held a device that strongly resembled a blood-pressure-cuff ensemble—except an inflatable pillow, rather than a cuff, resided at the end of the air hose.

Brendy stepped beside him and tried to concentrate on how he would open her door. Of course, that was nearly impossible when his dancing blue gaze silently adored her. She glanced at his lips, tilted in that boyish grin, and Brendy was nearly certain he whispered, "I want to kiss you." Yet his lips never moved.

Her heart began pattering as it had when they nearly did the jitterbug in the hallway. Nearby, a woodpecker hammered a tree, and Brendy started babbling in staccato rhythm with the bird.

"I was distracted because Sylvia called me on my cell. Sylvia, that's my part-time employee." Brendy waved her left hand. "Anyway, she called me on my cell about the time I was getting out. As soon as I shut the door, I knew my keys and purse were locked in." Her fingers flitted through the air. No matter how many times Brendy told herself to quit talking, her mouth kept moving. "But I had a teacher's meeting, so I decided to just wait until after the meeting to call."

Without a word, Zeke shifted his focus from her face to her left hand. His brows knitted, and a clever light twinkled in the baby blue eye that wasn't patched. When he got around to looking back into Brendy's face, she was breathless. "I, uh, I–I decided to take, er, to take it off. . . um. . .this morning," she stammered as a warm flush crept up her neck and burned her cheeks.

He winked and nodded, and they might as well have been sitting across from each other in algebra. "So I guess that means you might be free tomorrow night?" he queried.

Zeke reclined against the minivan and propped his arm upon the top. The lock was forgotten.

Brendy stopped herself short of a gape.

"The chamber of commerce is holding a chili supper to help raise money for beautifying downtown. I thought that maybe if you weren't busy. . ." He toyed with the strange mechanism in his hand, and Brendy sensed they had an audience.

She darted a glance to her grandchildren, who both observed this new man as if they didn't know whether he was friend or foe. Torn between the love from her past and the responsibilities of her present, Brendy wracked her brain for any reason she shouldn't accept Zeke's invitation. Her son Kent was scheduled to work at the hospital tomorrow night, and she debated whether to ask her mother to watch the children. At the age of seventy, Lila Angle could still work circles around Brendy some days. She seldom imposed upon her mom, despite the fact that Lila frequently offered her assistance. Perhaps the time had come to accept the help. Besides, Brendy needed a break. After today's teacher's conference, she was on the verge of despair over what to do with Pete.

"I'd *love* to go." As a gentle warmth tickled her tummy, Brendy wondered if she sounded a bit too enthusiastic.

Zeke's baritone laughter, warm as the east Texas

sunshine, dashed aside any worries. "Great! Then I'll pick you up about five-thirty; is that okay?"

Brendy looked at the scattered gravel, dared another glance at him, and tugged on an auburn curl. At once she felt like a coy sixteen year old accepting her first date. Her vague nod seemed all the answer Zeke needed.

"Good," he said. "Then it's a date."

"Hello–o–o, people!" Pete's abrupt interruption from the front of the van shattered the magical moment. "Some of us are tired of standing here."

Zeke's brow furrowed as he glanced toward the children, and Brendy thought about dissolving into an embarrassed heap. *"Pete!"* she exclaimed. "You're not supposed to address your elders like that. What is *wrong* with you?"

His bottom lip protruded while Pat walked around the van and slumped against her grandmother. A pathetic whimper reminded Brendy that she had others to consider besides herself—children who were hot and tired and ready to leave.

"I guess I *did* make the little guys stand in the sun, didn't I?" Zeke asked and directed a charming smile to Pete. "When I was growing up, after a long day at school, all I wanted to do was hit the couch and have myself some milk and cookies."

Pete eyed the friendly newcomer, and Brendy was almost certain he came close to a smile. Yet he hardened his lips and chose a glare instead. Pete hadn't been the same since his mother left, and Brendy wondered if he'd ever learn to trust again.

"This is called a Jiffy Jak." Zeke held up his interesting contraption for Brendy to see. "This little air pump inflates this pillow, like so." He pumped the ball, and Pat's attention was riveted upon the plastic pillow that began to expand. Brendy sneaked a glance toward Pete, who was trying to act disinterested.

"Here," he extended the instrument to Pat, "hold this for me. I need to get a few more things out of my van." Pat took the gadget, and Pete could stand the suspense no longer. He trudged around the vehicle and examined this new oddity called a Jiffy Jak.

Zeke retrieved a short bar and petite wooden wedge from his van. "Brendy, I'm going to pry your door open on the side with this." He held up the bar. "I'll place the wedge in the door first so nothing is scratched or bent. In the end, there will be a space just big enough for me to insert this little air bag. Then I'll inflate the air bag, which will give me a space in the door big enough to use this." He held up a long metal rod. "This is what I'll hit your lock with, and you'll be all free. It's as simple as one, two, three," he said.

"And it won't bend my door?" Brendy asked and hated that she sounded so doubtful.

"No, Ma'am." He raised three straight fingers. "Scout's honor."

"That's all I needed to hear." She lifted her chin as if she had the utmost confidence in his pledge.

Just as Zeke claimed, he had her van door opened in a few seconds. Pete even forgot to be hostile as he helped the locksmith return the fascinating tools to the van.

Finally, Zeke snapped his vehicle's sliding door in place. The kids tumbled into Brendy's van. Yet she hesitated to get in the vehicle as Zeke focused solely upon her.

When he spoke, the nuance of his voice suggested they were sharing the most intimate of secrets. "I'm really glad you called me," he muttered, and his heart was in his eye. Zeke reached toward her cheek and stopped. With an apologetic smile he dropped his hand to his side, and Brendy restrained herself from begging him to stroke her cheek anyway. She would have closed her eyes and leaned into his touch and maybe, just maybe, he would have kissed her.

"Stop it! Stop it! Stop it!" Pat screamed. "Grandmom, he's pulling my hair!"

"Well, she took my ruler!"

Brendy shook her head and dashed aside all those latent yearnings from years gone by. "I guess it's time for me to go," she said.

"Right." A ribbon of disappointment crossed Zeke's features. Features forever etched upon Brendy's heart. A straight, prominent nose, generous mouth, and high cheekbones. Everyone in his family said he took after his paternal grandfather, who was one-half Native American. Nevertheless, he'd inherited his mother's baby blues, which contrasted handsomely with his dark hair and skin tone. Only the thin white scar from ear to chin marred his mature features. Fleetingly, Brendy wondered if the scar was related to the problem with his eye. She started to ask but didn't. Maybe tomorrow evening he'd explain.

"I. . .guess I'll be seeing you tomorrow night, then?" he asked.

"Yes, tomorrow night," Brendy agreed and hated the thought of driving off and leaving him.

"Okay then, tomorrow night," he repeated.

Brendy made no move to depart. The years since they'd shared those last stolen kisses seemed to throb between them with the poignancy of long-lost love.

Some lonely voice deep within bade her linger with this man who still seemed so much a part of her. "Unless. . . ," Brendy began. She cast a furtive glance toward her grandchildren, who were jostling into their seats and snapping seat belts. "Unless you'd like to eat with us tonight." She spoke the words as soon as they entered her mind.

"I'd *love* to," Zeke said with the same eager acceptance she'd voiced.

"Great!" she said on a breathy note and leaned against the van to keep from collapsing. "I–I've still got to go back to the shop and work until five," she rushed on. "So, um, does six sound fine?"

"You bet," he agreed. "And, instead of you cooking, why don't I run by Stacy's Barbecue and pick up the works—diced beef, plenty of sauce, coleslaw, and potato salad. I'll even dart into the Wal-Mart Super Center and get us a bag of hamburger buns."

"But I don't mind cooking—"

"Nonsense," he said and shook his head in a manner that broached no argument. "You'll be tired—just like I will. Besides—" he threw in a sly wink—"if you make a mess in the kitchen, I'll feel obligated to help clean up." His face dropped into a piteous mope. "And I don't want to wash dishes half the night. Do you?"

Brendy giggled as if they were sharing straws over a soda at the Dairy Queen. "I've got paper plates and cups. Does that work?"

"Deal." Zeke extended his hand. Brendy inserted her hand into his. As she remembered, her fingers slid into his palm as though they were made for each other. The contact that started as a handshake soon turned to a caress, and Zeke's fingers stroked her skin. His hand trembled. Brendy caught her breath. Helplessly, she gazed into the soul that had once pledged his undying faith in her. This time, when he reached to touch her cheek, he didn't stop. As the backs of his fingers grazed her face, Brendy felt as if she were sucked into a tide of what-might-have-beens, all wrapped up in a warm sheath of what-could-bes. She closed her eyes and shamelessly tilted her head into his caress.

"Hello–o–o, people!" Pete's bellow shattered the moment.

Brendy's eyes popped open. Her shoulders slumped, and she whispered a remorseful, "I'm sorry. He's got a lot to be angry about. It's a long story. I'll explain tonight."

"Well, they've got to be hot in there," Zeke said and gazed across the sunbathed countryside full of rolling hills and plenty of pines. "Summer seems to think it's time to move on in—even though it *is* just the beginning of May." He squeezed her upper arm. "I'll see you in a bit. You take care of those kiddos, you hear?"

Brendy conjured her most dazzling smile and then

shamelessly hoped she knocked his socks off. "We'll look for you and your barbecue at six then."

"We'll be there!"

It wasn't until after Brendy flopped into the driver's seat, cranked the engine, and turned on the air-conditioner that she realized she hadn't paid Zeke for opening her door.

I'll write him a check tonight, she thought at the same time Pat's tentative voice pierced her romantic musings.

"Grandmom, who was that man?"

"He, uh, he's just a friend from a long time ago," she answered and waved as Zeke's van rolled in front of hers. Brendy started to put the vehicle in drive but stopped at her grandson's question.

"Are you going to marry him?" Pete accused.

She looked in the rearview mirror. "Pete Lane, whatever gave you *that* idea?" she asked and felt like nothing short of a Benedict Arnold. For Brendy *had* pondered those possibilities. She had pondered them all afternoon.

In response, Pete shrugged and slumped farther down into his seat.

"Because that's what happened with Mommy," Pat answered. Pete attempted to hit her. She glowered at her brother and continued to describe what Brendy suspected but had not yet been confirmed. "She kept meeting that man she said was just a friend. But he looked at her just like that man looked at you. And then she left us to go be with him. Are you going to leave us too?"

A stab of dread punctured Brendy's romantic musings. So, her daughter-in-law *had* met her boyfriend with the children present. From the start of that horrific separation and ultimate divorce, Brendy imagined the children might have witnessed their mom flirting with her boyfriend. Once again, Brendy wished the vixen were present so she could receive an overdue tongue-lashing from a livid mother-in-law.

She turned around and looked both children in the eyes. "Listen," she said, "nothing would *ever* make me leave you—*ever!* Understand?"

Pete's stern mouth relaxed a fraction, and Pat rubbed her nose. "Yes, Ma'am," the little girl answered as if by rote. Pete looked out the window. A cloud of uncertainty emanated from them both.

With a helpless shroud encompassing her, Brendy turned back around. Out of the corner of her eye, she caught a final glimpse of Zeke's van cruising up Corinth Road.

As she put the vehicle in gear and steered the van from the parking lot, a silent war raged within. She was no longer so certain she should have readily accepted Zeke's invitation for chili or even invited him for dinner tonight. Brendy glanced in her rearview mirror and wanted to weep over the blond-headed heartaches in the backseat. Indeed, her every decision now involved more than just her. Fleetingly she wondered if she had any business reliving a past that insisted she fantasize about the future. A future that belonged to her grandchildren.

Chapter *Four*

    he next two months
swelled into a sea of stolen moments, clandestine meet-
ings, and late-night dates. The children's welfare con-
sumed Brendy, and Zeke honored her request to keep
their relationship low-profile. Yet during that season of
getting reacquainted, Zeke told Brendy of Vietnam. . .of
his eye, his leg, the facial scar. . .of those awful days in
recovery. . .of his trip back home. . .of the rehab nurse
who became his wife. He proudly showed her pictures of
his twin sons, now living in Houston, both successful
businessmen; and he didn't bother to suppress the swell
in his voice when he spoke of his four grandchildren. He
also mentioned his wife's untimely death, although many

details were too painful to recount.

Likewise Brendy shared with Zeke. She told him of her marriage to Mack. . .of her daughter, a teacher living in Henderson. . .of the daughter's rowdy-yet-delightful boys. . .of her daughter-in-law's desertion. . .of her son's hectic work schedule. She even explained her struggle against bitterness toward her former daughter-in-law. And Brendy wept through the story of her husband's heart attack and how the small Texas town had mourned the death of the favored banker and churchman.

In the midst of all the sharing and romance and support, Brendy and Zeke discovered the balm of companionship, the essence of love, the promise of matrimony. So fiercely did they fan the flames of their long-lost love, Zeke decided the time had come to propose. Neither Brendy nor he were spring chickens, by any means. They both were lonely. They had never stopped loving each other. And each hinted that they believed God Himself was restoring unto them that which had been lost.

"So why wait?" Zeke whispered to himself that Saturday night as he slid from his van on El Paso Street. He walked across the cracked sidewalk toward Brendy's house—a rambling two-story Victorian affair with more rooms than she could use. In precise fashion, he answered his own question. *Actually, I can think of two reasons to wait to get married. Their names are Pat and Pete.*

Zeke clutched the stuffed Wal-Mart bag and slowed his uneven gait. He eyed the remodeled white house with fashionable blue trim that oozed early twentieth-century character. Zeke imagined Brendy's grandchildren skipping along the wraparound porch—a porch that welcomed all with the added appeal of hanging ferns. The porch swing even danced in the hot breeze as if Pat and Pete were enjoying the ride.

Zeke shook his head and wondered what he was going to have to do to win them over. While they hadn't been overtly hostile by any means, the two still scruti-nized him with the suspicion of the betrayed—and that was only on the occasions they'd *known* he was going out with their grandmother. He could only imagine their reaction if they understood the wealth of time he and Brendy were enjoying together.

The night that Zeke had taken Brendy to the cham-ber of commerce chili supper, Brendy explained the children's situation and even detailed the conversation at the school. "I think they're afraid you're going to take me away," she'd explained.

"I just might," Zeke had teased with an exaggerated wink and marveled at his own bravado so early in their renewed relationship.

"Oh, stop it!" Brendy slapped at his arm as if they were still going steady. "We need to be cautious about this; that's all I'm saying. I want to make sure the kids feel as secure as possible under the circumstances."

So we've been cautious, he thought. *If you call sneaking out for midnight drives cautious.* Zeke yawned and covered his mouth. "Something's got to change," he said, "or this is going to kill me."

When Brendy invited him over to dine with her grandchildren and son, they both hoped that the children might grow accustomed to the idea of their grandmother's suitor. Yet a low rumble of thunder from the west that predicted a much-needed rain also sent a ripple of dread through Zeke.

Pete was a hard kid to reach and didn't mind sassing Brendy. Over the last couple of months, Zeke decided Pete's most pressing need was a firmer hand with discipline. The person to offer that security should have been his father. Yet Kent Lane, an RN, worked a double shift many days at the hospital. Zeke even suspected that the young man he'd only met in passing might be trying to escape his problems rather than face them. That left Brendy bearing the brunt of the responsibilities. Those issues aside, he often wondered if his attempts to win Pete would prove a loss.

As a redbird zipped between him and the house, the July heat, oppressive and humid, weighed upon him. Indeed, summer was at it's height, and Zeke's thigh even perspired against his prosthesis. Mere feet from the porch steps, he maneuvered around Pat's Barbie bicycle, which had been dropped and left in the walkway.

Now that little girl was a different story. While Pete's distrust was more overt, Pat was most apt to cling to Brendy's leg and stare at Zeke with owl-like blue eyes— too big for her face, too wise for her years.

Zeke clutched the shopping bag all the tighter, climbed up the porch steps, and knocked on the front door. He was hoping maybe the toys he'd just bought would convince the children he was friend, not foe. Usually, he didn't have to resort to such measures with little ones. His own grandchildren often begged to come stay with their Pa Blake. But he was falling deeper in love with Brendy by the day and wanted nothing more than to place his wedding band on her finger. Indeed, Zeke was a desperate man—desperate enough to prowl the aisles of Discount City until he found the perfect gifts, a new ball glove for Pete and a Barbie for Pat.

He repeated the knock, this time louder, and strained to hear signs of life. At last, the tromping of small feet paused near the door. Pete called, "Who is it?"

"It's. . ." Zeke paused and wondered if there was another name he could encourage the children to call him besides "Mr. Blake." The formality of the surname suggested he was not a part of their family. "It's Mr. Zeke," he said and hoped one day to change that to Grandpa Zeke—and then maybe just Grandpa.

The door creaked open, and Pete observed him through the screen. Pat hovered behind as usual, and Zeke felt as if he were a bungling nineteen year old, being examined by a prospective father-in-law. *The years certainly have a way of changing the roles,* he thought with a hint of frantic humor.

"Grandmom's in the kitchen," Pete said as he unlatched the screen door. "We'll tell her you're here."

Before Zeke had the chance to even mention his gifts, the straw-headed twosome turned as one and darted from the doorway. Zeke opened the screen door that squawked on resistant hinges. Before the night was over, he planned to retrieve the can of WD40 from his van and spray those hinges. The smell of smothered steak sent a growl through his belly as Zeke secured the door and meandered into the den. The spacious room with high ceilings and a marble fireplace appeared to have once been a decorator's paradise. Yet the shades on the brass lamps now hung crooked. A tea stain ringed the mauve love seat. And the center of the floor looked like a glorified playroom, replete with building blocks scattered all the way to the recliner, where he gratefully dropped.

Shaking his head, Zeke remembered the days of raising kids. In fact, he and his wife decided there was no use buying new furniture until the boys were grown. The country decor Zeke now used had been the product of Madeline's shopping spree the week their nest was officially empty. Yet she hadn't lived much longer to enjoy it.

A melancholic ache pierced Zeke's heart as he flipped the recliner's handle and relaxed into the chair's comforting folds. He hadn't thought of Maddy's untimely departure in days. And he thanked the Lord that this time the pain wasn't quite as sharp.

As he gazed toward the gurgling goldfish tank atop a Queen Anne side table, his drowsy mind drifted to Brendy. An evening listening to her melodious voice and touching her soft face promised the balm to heal all hurts, all disappointments, all lost dreams. His heavy eyes closed, and he pondered the possibilities of making her a permanent part of his world. . .waking to her laughter, sharing her love for gourmet coffee and chocolate, delighting in the union that would make them man and wife.

In the middle of his fantasies, Zeke's skin crawled

like it had the day those checkers kings were giving him the once-over. He barely lifted one eyelid and attempted to validate his suspicions of two short spies. To his left, he noted a couple of half-faces peering around a hallway door. Both had silky, blond hair, light tans, and keen blue eyes. Neither made a sound.

Zeke struggled to contain his amusement over the intensity of their gazes and hoped this might be the beginning of a friendship. "Hi, Pete and Pat," he said without a move. "Come on in."

With a jerk, the youngsters disappeared. Zeke kept watching. After a couple of minutes they came back. He figured his eyes, barely opened, appeared to be closed to the kids. He could only imagine their minds racing with how he could see them. He fumbled for the Wal-Mart bag and found it near the recliner's handle. "I brought you guys some toys." He lifted the bag yet didn't alter his position.

Pete's face disappeared again, but Pat crept out and stood in the doorway. Her face glowed with hesitant curiosity, and she inserted her index finger into her mouth. Zeke nearly roared with victory. He opened his eyes and slowly lowered the recliner's leg rest. As he was floundering with the bag, a hand reached out and tugged on the back of Pat's short set. She stumbled from sight.

Zeke's momentary victory deflated to despair when he caught a snatch of their hushed, yet urgent, argument. "But I want to see my toy," Pat's little voice pleaded.

"It's a trick! Don't you see?" Pete reasoned. "Now we're going back out there and telling him. . ."

The rest jumbled into urgent hissing, and Zeke peered into the blue plastic bag. The gifts he so hoped would speak his heart now seemed foolish and trite. He dug to the bottom in search of the receipt and tucked it into the pocket of his dress shirt. *Looks like I might be returning these,* he groused. Zeke patted the shirt pocket on a final note and felt the bulge of the tiny chain he'd placed there before leaving home.

Somehow in the rush and thrill of this raging romance, Zeke had failed to mention the key he still owned. Only when he'd seen the locket around Brendy's neck yesterday had he recalled that he placed the key in the porcelain dish on his dresser. Zeke had planned to give her the key tonight after dinner—when he proposed. He smiled and hoped the locket still opened after all these years.

A movement near the doorway diverted his mind back to the present problem—two motherless children who looked at him like he was the boogeyman. Pat hedged into the living room with Pete close behind. Her head bowed and lips pursed, she stopped so abruptly that Pete ran into her.

Zeke clasped the store bag and tried to decide whether to hold firm to the front line or retreat.

"We don't want your gifts," Pete proclaimed as if he were a secret agent rejecting the assistance of the enemy.

Zeke's shoulders slumped, and he grappled for something to say—anything. Despite all his good intentions, his frustration mounted to aggravation. The child's torn jeans and smudged T-shirt looked like he'd been duking it out with the boy next door. And Zeke wondered if the child thought he could bully him as well. *Not in my lifetime,* he thought with a twist of his lips. *I'm tired of being pushed around by a half-pint!*

"You're just trying to fool us!" Pete accused, his brows knitted.

"No, I'm not!" Zeke denied, and every child-rearing book he'd ever read disappeared from memory.

The boy's chest protruded as if he were bravely enduring the enemy's camp. "You want us to forget what you're doin'."

"Exactly *what* am I doing?" Zeke pulled on his pants leg and leaned forward. He told himself he really wasn't heading into hand-to-hand combat. Still, his hackles rose as if he were facing the front line in Vietnam.

"It's about Grandmom!"

Pat retreated to Pete's side and hovered behind him. Zeke wondered if the little girl were trying to get out of the line of fire.

"You're always botherin' her." A furious flush tinged Pete's tanned cheeks.

"Bothering her?" Zeke responded and felt like a brainless parrot.

"She spends all her time fixin' up for you!" He stomped his foot.

"Sounds to me like she *likes* me to bother her, then," Zeke claimed and narrowed an eye at the boy. The army never taught him how to deal with enemies this short.

"And she cooks special stuff for you too." As if to punctuate the child's claim, the scent of freshly brewing coffee mingled with the smell of smothered steak. Like a warrior upon the brink of victory, Pete crossed his arms and glowered at his foe.

Zeke, grappling for a defense tactic, dashed a glance at Pat, whose giant orbs drifted toward the store bag now at Zeke's feet. He didn't stop the slow smile from lifting the corners of his mouth. "I got you a Barbie set," Zeke explained and focused on the little girl. He withdrew the doll, replete with three changes of clothing and extended it toward Pat.

"Don't take it!" Pete commanded like a desperate general. He turned on Zeke and hurled a stream of words like the fire of a machine gun. "You think you can make us like you with gifts, but it *won't work!*"

"Pete Lane!" Brendy's breathless gasp reverberated around the room. Zeke looked at the woman of his dreams. Flour dusted her floral apron and copper curls. Her rounded eyes, at first bewildered, ultimately glared bullets at her grandson. Any minute, Zeke expected her to crouch, run forward, and pluck him from the enemy's mortal trap.

Zeke didn't give her the chance. Instead, he stood and moved to her side. He knew a good rescue team member when he saw one, and Brendy Lane was as skillful as *any* he'd welcomed in the army.

Chapter *Five*

*B*rendy scrutinized her grandson's hostile face. A barrage of options hurled themselves at her. She didn't know whether to send him to his room, try to ease his fears, or cry. Brendy felt that the more she tried to encourage Pete to like Zeke, the more he resisted. The more he resisted, the more Pat was likewise hindered. Last night, when she told Pete that Zeke was coming for dinner, he stomped to his room, slammed the door, and didn't come out for an hour. This morning at two A.M., a sobbing Pat crawled into bed with Brendy. She claimed she'd had a nightmare in which Brendy threw her away. And Brendy, groggy and angry, had wanted to share a piece of her mind with that mother of Pat's.

As she stroked her apron, Zeke placed a hand in the small of her back and leaned toward her. "Let's go into the kitchen," he whispered, and his mint-tinged breath tickled her nose. "I'll help you finish."

"But. . ." Brendy gazed into Zeke's eyes. The patch was long gone, and he now wore the prosthesis. The blue orb so resembled his other eye that Brendy had to remind herself that he couldn't see out of it.

Zeke's response was a jerk of his head toward the kitchen. "I have a plan," he mumbled, as if they were dropping behind enemy lines and pausing to orchestrate their strategy.

With a nod Brendy led the way through the dining area and into the room she adored because cooking was one of her favorite pastimes. The smell of smothered steak, candied carrots, tomato basil soup, steamed wild rice, and broccoli made even *her* mouth water. Before turning to Zeke, Brendy grabbed a spoon, stirred the steaming carrots, and flipped off the electric burner.

His eyes rolled and he clutched his gut. "Forget the kids. Let's just *eat!*"

Brendy giggled as a warm glow infused her being. "Here." She lifted the lid off of a pot of broccoli and cheese, dipped a sample into a bowl and extended it to

Zeke. "You can eat while we talk."

"A woman after my own heart," Zeke purred. He set the plastic bag on the kitchen counter, cluttered with a cutting board and carrot tops, and he took the bowl without a hint of protest. His gaze trailed toward the neckline of Brendy's denim jumper, and he broke into a smile that would have stopped traffic in downtown Dallas.

She touched the locket hanging around her neck by a new gold chain. Brendy had taken the piece to Lang's Jewelry last week to have it polished. To her surprise, the jeweler told her the heart was actually ten-carat gold. The chain, however, was only gold plated and too far gone to be salvaged.

"It's time for me to set the table," Brendy said and dared to dash him a saucy wink. Her womanly intuition suggested that Zeke was on the verge of proposing. She wanted tonight to be extra special, and she even set out her best crystal, along with polished silver and Noritake china. Once before, she had squandered an opportunity with Zeke. Brendy was not about to do that again. Therefore, she had designed this evening to show how deeply their renewed love permeated her heart.

"Wait!" Zeke snared her hand and tugged her back to his side. "We need to talk about *them,*" he insisted and jerked his head toward the living room.

"Oh! I'm so scattered I was distracted the minute I got in here. I've lived from one crisis to another today, and I'm starting to get ditzy." She touched her temple. "Maybe it's just that, these days, Pete lives from one blowup to the next, and I'm starting to tune it all out once I leave the room." She shrugged and shook her head. "I guess maybe it's just my way of surviving all this."

"Here's what I think," Zeke said. "You might be onto something smart. Let's ignore his negative behavior. I think if we major on it, we're validating it. Let's continue with our plans, and when he erupts we'll just smile and keep on truckin'."

Brendy concentrated on his advice, and the longer he talked, the more the idea made sense. "I guess it's like ignoring a child who throws a fit," she said. "What they want is attention, and they're trying to get it no matter what. If you ignore the fit, then they aren't successful."

"Exactly."

Brendy nodded and examined the stack of pots and pans piled in the kitchen sink. "Might work," she said and toyed with the hem of her apron. "And maybe we haven't been doing anybody a favor by sneaking around so much. Maybe the thing that would be best for the children is to see us together as often as possible. Eventually, they'll *have* to realize you're safe, and I'm not going anywhere."

Zeke set the bowl of broccoli on the table and gripped Brendy's upper arms. "Those are the most beautiful words I've ever heard," he said as if she'd just uttered a melodic poem. "This crazy courtship is going to *kill* me if we have to keep sneaking around. I can't do very many more late-night trips to the Dairy Queen." His forehead wrinkled, and the dark circles under his eyes validated his claims.

A burst of laughter erupted from Brendy, and she laid a hand on his face. "I'm tired too," she admitted and massaged the small of her back. Brendy didn't elaborate on the fact that she was not only physically exhausted, but mentally and emotionally spent as well. Add to that the perpetual spiritual battle against bitterness toward her daughter-in-law, and Brendy wasn't certain she could take another crisis without falling apart.

He pulled her into the circle of his strong arms, and Brendy relished the faint scent of Brut. She believed he'd worn that aftershave when they were dating. Brendy rested her cheek on his chest, closed her eyes, and imagined them standing near the weeping willow tree at Lake Jacksonville. They were both eighteen. . .carefree. . .and looking forward to a fulfilling life together. If she fantasized enough, Brendy could nearly convince herself she really didn't have the responsibility of two heartbroken grandchildren—that she and Zeke could elope any day they wished.

The creak of the hardwood floor preceded someone clearing his throat. Brendy jumped away from Zeke as if she'd been caught in the most heinous of crimes. She glanced toward her son who entered from the hallway, toweling his hair dry. Kent offered Zeke a cool greeting, and Brendy couldn't deny the trace of caution in her son's eyes. She busied herself around the stove as if she were a teenager caught necking on the front porch.

Kent moved toward his mom and paused by the oven, as if he were ravenous. The look on his face said enough. Brendy smiled up at him. "Dinner's on in about five minutes," she explained.

"Great. I'm starving," he admitted and eyed the mound of wild rice sitting in the middle of the stove. He draped the damp towel around his neck, and the ends settled upon the front of his Jacksonville College tank top.

Everyone said Kent was the spit and image of his father—the blond hair, the full lips, the brown eyes, the developed physique, lean yet muscular. All that was a big part of the problem. Kent had had his share of ladies after him from the time he was in junior high school. Brendy often wondered why, of all the sensible girls he could have chosen, he wound up with the one who was fickle, foolish, and more in love with herself than her family.

"Where are the kids?" Kent asked.

"I think they're in the living room," Brendy said and cast a cautious gaze to Zeke.

"No. I just checked in there," Kent said. "I couldn't find them anywhere in the house."

"Think they went outside?" Zeke asked.

Kent moved to the back door and tugged aside the cheerful checked curtain, the color of currants. "Yep. That's exactly where they are. They're playing in the dirt."

"Oh, no, not now," Brendy moaned. "Dinner's only five minutes away." She moved toward the doorway. "I'll call—"

Zeke gripped her arm and shook his head. "Let *him* take care of it," he whispered. "They're *his* kids."

Brendy blinked and stared at Zeke as the implications of his words penetrated her scattered mind. In a instant, she relived the tension since Kent's wife deserted the family. From the day her son moved in and started working insane hours, she'd been both mother and father to those children. Even when Kent was around, she stepped forward to parent them. Maybe Zeke was right. Perhaps the time *had* come to enable her son to be their father.

"On second thought," Brendy said, "I really need to set the table, Kent. I'll let you go ahead and get them cleaned up, okay?"

"Sure," he said and opened the back door.

Zeke gave Brendy the thumbs-up sign and then said, "What can I do to help?"

Zeke settled at the oval oak table he and Brendy had set. He admired her ability to create divine dinners and make the spread look like a centerfold from *Good Housekeeping*. Zeke knew for a fact that her love of cooking began in the kitchen with her mother, who never minded when Brendy brought him home for dinner. During their high school courtship, Brendy often sat across the table smiling at her beau while her brothers silently eyed him, as Kent was doing now.

One Saturday evening Brendy even stated, "I helped Mamma make the shrimp gumbo." A monstrous stainless steel pot had commanded the table's center and issued the exotic aromas of peppers, onions, celery, and garlic. Brendy's mom was a Cajun girl from southwest Louisiana, and one of Brendy's favorite dishes was still gumbo.

But tonight she had prepared a different kind of feast. Instead of gumbo, a steaming bowl of tomato basil soup claimed the center of each of the exquisite china plates.

She even remembered to place a sprig of parsley in the center of each bowl. Zeke gazed upon the spread and realized he had not yet tasted a bite of the broccoli and cheese that Brendy had spooned out for him earlier. He spotted the broccoli, residing in a crystal bowl on Kent's side of the table, and decided to get an extra helping when it came his way.

Meanwhile, Zeke toyed with the tiny key he'd retrieved from the pocket of his dress shirt. Seeing that locket had made him decide a different way to give the key to Brendy. He hoped she'd be as delighted with his clever plan as he was. Zeke had never considered himself a romantic, but lately he was doing well by anybody's standards. Brendy hinted a time or two that if she ever got married again she would prefer a simple gold band, so Zeke had refrained from buying an engagement ring. However, he wanted to do *something* to commemorate the moment. The key was his answer.

"Where are Pete and Pat?" Brendy asked. She placed a basket of home-baked rolls near the smothered steak; then she claimed her spot between Zeke and her son.

Kent rose from his high-backed chair. "I left them washing their hands and told them to make it quick," he mumbled.

He hadn't taken one step before the two children

hurried from the hallway and clambered into their chairs. "There they are," Kent said and dashed a smile as the two sat across from each other. Pete, settling beside Zeke, smiled back as if he'd received the best prize of the whole evening.

At once, Zeke figured Pete would turn down a whole truckload of ball gloves for a little time with his father. His heart went out to the troubled eight year old, and he despaired that he would ever break through the child's barriers.

Brendy, at the head of the table, looked at Zeke and said, "Would you give thanks?"

He smiled at Pete and Pat, who returned his appraisal with near-angelic gazes. Suspicion set bells of caution pealing through Zeke's mind—much like the shriek of a horn during an enemy's raid. Pat wiggled like she had a bug in her drawers, and Pete shot her a stare that would freeze a bonfire. Zeke glanced to Brendy. One of her finely penciled brows cocked upward, and a glimmer of speculation marred her jade green eyes. Zeke's quick look toward Kent revealed a father who was innocently placid.

Or maybe so out of touch he's oblivious, Zeke thought, then scolded himself. *I'm probably just imagining things.* With no more deliberation, he decided to go ahead and pray. Out of habit, he began reaching to hold hands and stopped himself from reaching toward Pete. *He probably would rather eat a skunk than hold my hand,* he thought.

With the key in his palm, he extended his hand toward Brendy. When she slipped her hand in his, the symbol of their past warmed between them. He detected her faint gasp as he began the simple prayer. When he pronounced a resounding "Amen," he cut her a glance and winked at her.

She smiled back, examined the tiny scrap of metal, and looked at him as if he were the most wonderful man alive. On an impulse Zeke nearly stole a kiss but thought better of it—especially when he noticed Kent eyeing him like a disapproving father-in-law. While Zeke wanted to run around the room and shout, *I'm in love! I'm in love!* he chose instead to refrain and eat his soup like a respectable guest.

First, he indulged in a slow drink of the iced tea from his crystal goblet and reveled in the cool southern sweetness. When he replaced the goblet, Zeke noted the children were attacking their soup with more urgency than he expected—especially considering they were kids and this *was* tomato basil. Indeed, their little faces were nearly buried in the creamy liquid. Zeke's gaze met Brendy's, and the two of them shared a private communication as strong as any spoken word. The suspicions from before the prayer were surfacing again. Those two were up to something.

Zeke decided his best bet was to eat and mind his own business. As he prepared to remove the sprig of parsley from the center of his soup, he noted that the parsley had disappeared. *That's strange,* he thought. With an inward shrug, Ezekiel dipped his soup spoon into the creamy mixture, and the parsley surfaced with an extra bit of protein. In fact, a writhing night crawler the size of a small snake hung on either side of his spoon.

"Oh, my word!" Brendy gasped.

A deathly silence settled upon the table—a silence broken only by the clank of the children's spoons against their bowls as they continued gobbling the soup at lightning speed. After the initial surprise, Zeke eyed the creature and debated his options. His recent speech to Brendy about ignoring negative behavior flitted through his mind, yet Zeke somehow couldn't bring himself to pretend this incident hadn't happen.

As silence reigned, the worm turned until it lay across the handle's shank. Like a snake captured on a hook, the poor thing had maneuvered to a position of hanging equal parts of head and tail on either side. No amount of squeezing its tiny muscles made a difference.

Zeke eyed the intruder and jumped into a dialogue he'd never planned. "Well, I'll be switched. Where you been, Willie?" he exclaimed. "I've looked all over the house for you." Zeke extended the night crawler toward Pete.

Pat stopped eating and, with a horror-struck expression, stared as Pete scooted to the far edge of his seat. Sensing he had the element of surprise to his favor, Zeke moved the spoon to his ear and pretended to be listening. "What's that you say?" he asked, and his attention rested upon Kent, who had begun a low snicker.

Pete gaped at Zeke, his face covered with a mixture of dread and shock. Certainly, this turn of events was obviously *not* what he had anticipated.

Zeke, pointing at Willie, leaned toward Pete and whispered, "He says he wants to be your friend, Pete." He stopped and held up a hand. "No, wait! Now he's saying that's *not* what he meant. He's saying he wants you to *eat* him."

Kent's snickers exploded into outright laughter as Zeke stood and held the spoon over Pete's head. The worm sashayed back and forth as if he were in the midst of a delightful swing. The child looked up and screamed, "Nooooooo!" at the same time the worm slipped off the spoon. The creature landed with a splat of tomato soup on Pete's upper lip and flopped into his mouth.

An ominous hush claimed the table for but a second as the realization of what just happened sank into one and all.

About the time Zeke started to stutter out an apology, Pete spat the worm into his soup bowl and began gagging. His face grew scarlet as the gags turned to near-convulsions.

Pat screamed as if Zeke were threatening to cut off her head. She yanked on her hair and started howling. "Don't let him, Grandmom! Don't let that mean man make me eat a worm!" A hysterical fit followed with such shrieks that anyone from miles around would assume the child was being beaten to death.

Brendy rose from her chair and scooped the little girl into her arms. She scowled at Zeke and crammed the locket key back into his hand. "How *could* you?" she demanded.

"Wait a minute!" Zeke responded. "I didn't do that on purpose. You should know me well enough to know it was an accident. I didn't mean any harm. I wasn't going to—"

A desperate gurgling interrupted his disclaimer, and Zeke looked at Pete. The child was chugalugging his crystal goblet full of tea as Pat snuggled her head against Brendy's shoulder and whimpered. Her face flushing, Brendy clutched her granddaughter, pushed past Zeke, and neared Pete.

Zeke, ready to convince the world of his innocence, silently beseeched Kent with the most virtuous expression he could muster. But Kent didn't even notice. He was doubled over his soup, laughing so hard he was heaving. Brendy cleared her throat and cut another glare to her son. After catching her eye, Kent possessed the decency to stumble from his chair toward the kitchen. As Pete doused his mouth with the remaining tea, Zeke decided he was safer with Kent than Brendy.

Yet the minute he stepped into the kitchen, he knew he had miscalculated the equation. Kent collapsed against the kitchen door and held his gut. "I can't stop," he gasped. The spacious kitchen reverberated with guffaws as Kent swiped at the tears streaming his cheeks.

Despite Zeke's desire to remain serious, Kent's laughter proved contagious. He started with a mild chortle. Zeke scratched the back of his neck and tried to compose himself in the face of unexpected hilarity. Indeed, the more he thought about Pete's expression when he realized a worm was in his mouth, the less self-control he possessed.

"Did you see the look on his face?" Kent gasped.

And Zeke could contain his laughter no longer. "It was like—like something on *The Little Rascals,*" he finally said and rested his heaving body against the cluttered counter.

Kent pointed at Zeke and nodded his head. "Exactly. All—all he needed was a cowlick, sticking straight up, and—"

"He could be Alfalfa!" Zeke finished. He pressed his eyes and told himself he needed to get a grip, but the more he tried, the harder he laughed.

That is, until Brendy came into the kitchen. "Excuse me!" she demanded, and both men went rigid as if snapping to attention for the most demanding of generals.

Chapter *Six*

*W*iping his eyes, Zeke was reminded of a mother bear ready to take on an army for the cause of her cubs. *Oh boy,* he thought, *we're heading for trouble.*

First, Brendy looked at her son and snarled, "If you have no more respect for your children than this—"

"Mom," Kent said and raised his hand, "he had it coming." A low-key chuckle rumbled out. "If he's going to put worms in people's soup, then he should expect some consequences. Maybe—" He pressed his lips together until they wobbled. "Maybe it was an act of God!" The very idea hurled both men into another fit of hilarity.

"Go to your room!" Brendy yelled.

"What?" Kent responded and pointed to his chest. "I'm nearly thirty and those kids are *mine!*"

"Fine, then," Brendy growled. "Go somewhere else where they can't hear you laughing them to scorn! This is probably the most humiliating moment of Pete's life. The last thing he needs is—"

"If you think he's humiliated, think how the worm must feel," Kent said and howled at his own joke.

Struggling to contain his laughter, Zeke turned his back, crammed his knuckles against his lips, and hunched his shoulders.

Zeke figured the joke only added fuel to Brendy's rage, but he couldn't stop the snickers. When he felt her turn on him, he decided he'd rather face the fire than take a hit from behind. As he swiveled, Zeke encountered the worst feminine weapon of them all—*tears!* He groaned within and knew he'd just lost the battle.

"And you!" Brendy pointed at his nose. "A grown man, a grandfather yourself, terrifying—"

"Wait a minute, Honey," Zeke said and rubbed the key between his forefinger and thumb. "You know I didn't do any of that on purpose. It was an *accident.*" The back door slammed. Zeke glanced over his shoulder. Kent had left him to face the interrogation alone. *A fine backup you turned out to be,* he thought.

"Well, the least you could do is have the decency not to laugh at them. They've been through enough already without—" She stopped and scrubbed at her eyes.

"Ah, Brendy," Zeke said and tried to place his arms around her.

"No!" She pushed him away and shook her head. "I think it would be best right now for you to just *go home!*"

"What? But I haven't even eaten!" Despite the upheaval, his stomach rumbled.

She crossed her arms. "Just leave," she repeated and pointed toward the door through which Kent had exited.

Mutely, Zeke extended the key toward her in an attempt to at least symbolize a future reconciliation.

"No." She pushed his hand away. Her copper curls swayed around her cheeks. Her chin jutted forward.

And Zeke knew arguing with her would be like trying to argue with a rabid bulldog. Never one to back down from a challenge, he decided to argue anyway. He wasn't afraid of bulldogs and never had been. "Brendy, I think you're overreacting here," he began on a serious note. "It was just a *worm.*" He bit down hard on the end of his tongue as he recalled Pete's chugalugging the tea.

"J–just a worm?" She pointed toward the dining room. "Pat is scared stiff you're going to make her eat one too! She even had a nightmare last night, Zeke! She dreamed I threw her away! She's worried sick that I'm going to choose you over her, and now she'll probably have nightmares about you forcing worms down her throat!"

"Why didn't you *tell* me about her dream?" he asked. "I didn't have to come tonight if—"

"Because. . .because. . ." Brendy moved toward the stove and placed a hand on the ledge. "Because I thought—thought that maybe we could work through it all. But now, I just don't know," she agonized. Twining her fingers together, she pivoted to face him again. "You and I both know this is about much. . .much more than just tonight, Ezekiel!" She took a deep breath, fumbled with the clasp on the locket, and Zeke's heart nearly hit his feet. "It's about the well-being of two tormented little souls who've been abandoned once." The locket hung from her fingers and sashayed between them like a pendulum ticking off the seconds until their relationship was over. "And I can't stand the thought of them being abandoned again. I just can't!" she wheezed out.

"Who said anything about abandoning them?" he reasoned. "I can move in here! We'll all be one happy family."

"Yeah, us and the worms!" she huffed and tossed the locket at him.

Zeke caught it, and the scrap of gold seemed as cold as ice. "Well, I'm not planning on any more worms," he said and couldn't quite believe Brendy was actually breaking up with him.

"I was crazy to think this would work." She shook her head as cascades of moisture christened her cheeks.

"But, Brendy. . ."

"The thing that's important here, Zeke Blake, is those children." She pointed toward the dining room again.

Zeke looked past her to see one of Pete's eyes peering around the facing. *Déjà vu,* he thought and detected a glimmer of triumph in the child's eye.

"And I cannot allow them to suffer due to my own selfishness."

"Suffer?" Zeke squeaked. "The person who's suffering here is *me!*" He ground all five fingers against his chest and couldn't quite absorb the pain. Zeke suspected that would all come later. "I'll tell you what's happening, Brendy Lane," he added and squared his shoulders. That little scamp might *think* he was winning, but Ezekiel Blake didn't plan to go down without a fight. "I'll tell you what's happening," he repeated with deliberation. "That child is ruling your life and you're letting him. He gets what he wants anytime he wants, and you think because he's—he's 'injured'—" Zeke drew invisible quote marks in midair—"that he shouldn't be disciplined."

"I discipline him," she shot back.

"Not like he needs!" Zeke boomed. "I've seen enough to know—"

"This is not the army!" she declared.

"Nobody said it *should* be." Zeke raised both hands. "I just don't think it's right to reward a child for a prank by running off the victim."

"Oh, so now *you're* the victim." She crossed her arms and raised her eyebrows.

"Well, yeah! That *was* my soup!"

"Grandmom," Pete said from the doorway, "Pat's cryin' again."

Without a word Brendy turned toward the dining room. When she passed through the doorway, Pete popped his head around the facing and stuck his tongue out at Zeke. His pug nose crinkled, and his cherry red lips formed a perfect "o" around that pink tongue.

A flash of heat exploded from Zeke's gut, and he took a step toward the brat. "Why, you little. . ."

With a yelp, Pete ran after his grandmother, and Zeke decided to stomp out before he did something he would later regret. No sooner had the door banged after him than he nearly ran over Kent. The young man stood with his hands in his pockets, gazing at the row of pine trees along the backyard fence. Zeke resisted projecting his ire for Pete's behavior upon Kent, but the temptation nearly proved too strong. He came within a breath of blurting, *That imp you call your son just stuck his tongue out at me!* Yet Kent spoke before Zeke opened his mouth.

"Mom's really stressed out," he said without ever looking at Zeke.

"Yep," Zeke said, and the simple response hid his exasperation. He settled onto his good leg and wished the mosquitoes weren't so fond of humid climates. He swatted at one of the pests already nipping at his arm and figured he'd be sweating like a sow by the time the next mosquito struck. The clouds that had been on the horizon when he arrived were now boiling across the sky. About the time Zeke was ready to tell Kent the time had come to be the father his children needed, a particularly nasty cloud blotted out the sun and offered a hint of relief from the evening heat.

"I guess. . ." Kent rubbed his hands together and cut a look at Zeke. "I guess I've been leaving most of, well, everything to her," he said.

"Yep," Zeke agreed and decided this might be one of the easiest conversations in which he'd ever participated. As his irritation began to wane, he examined the locket against his palm and thought about throwing the thing away. Zeke didn't want the golden heart around the house, tormenting him every time he saw it. And he sure wasn't going to be sentimental enough to keep the locket *or* key this time. Perhaps Brendy was right. Maybe they were both foolhardy to think they could impose their relationship of the past upon the problems of the present.

"Maybe I should give her some time off," Kent mused and noticed the gold glimmering against Zeke's callused palm. "Did she, like, break up with you?" he blurted.

"Yep," Zeke answered.

"Oh, man, I'm so sorry." Wide-eyed, Kent looked squarely into Zeke's face. For the first time Zeke sensed the young man saw him—actually saw him—as more than just an irritation in his life.

Yeah, I'm a real human being just like you are, Zeke wanted to say. *And I hurt just like you did when your wife left you.* Nevertheless, the hollow spot in his heart offered only numbness; and Ezekiel hoped he didn't start hurting— *really hurting*—until he got home.

"She's just mad right now," Kent said on a consoling note. "She'll get over it."

This time, Zeke couldn't answer "yep." Indeed, all his *yeps* were gone. He sighed and trudged past Kent. "I guess I'll head on over to the Sonic and get me a hamburger," he mumbled. The thought of fast food after seeing Brendy's meal was anticlimactic, to say the least.

"Wait!" Kent grabbed his arm. "Wait here—just a minute." He held up his finger. "I'll go in and fix you the best take-home meal you've ever had. I know where Mom keeps the paper plates. She's got some really *big* ones too." He produced a sizable oval with his hands.

Zeke figured the decent thing to do was politely decline, but his stomach thought otherwise. "Okay," he heard himself say. "And go heavy on the steak and broccoli, will ya?"

"Sure thing."

Kent was as good as his word. He came back in a jiffy with a plate piled high and covered with Saran Wrap. The curtain on the back door inched aside as if someone were checking on him. Zeke wondered if Brendy helped with the platter. He decided her helping was merely the humanitarian thing to do. After all, he was now a prisoner of war, banished from the home he wanted to be a part of. Even POWs deserved to eat.

"I appreciate you, Kent," Zeke said. "I really do."

"No problem." He laid a hand on Zeke's shoulders. "Sometimes, we men need to stick together." He smiled, and the two made eye contact long enough to remember the worm splattering tomato soup on Pete's upper lip, then flopping into his mouth. Both men burst into a spontaneous guffaw.

"He really looked just like Alfalfa." Zeke coughed over the words.

"I'll never forget that as long as I live." Kent groaned. "I think my stomach's probably going to be sore tomorrow."

Narrowing his eyes, Zeke decided that since they were doing all this male bonding he ought to usher in a heavy dose of brutal honesty. "Well, put this one in your hopper," he added, "and it's really not funny."

"Okay, what?" Kent asked.

"Pete just stuck his tongue out at me."

"No way!" Kent's heavy brows furrowed over astonished eyes.

"Yep," Zeke said. "He heard your mother tell me to get lost, and I guess he figured he'd won."

"Did Mom see him?"

"Nope. He made sure she couldn't see. But. . ." Zeke nudged a rock with the tip of his boot.

"What?" Kent prompted. "Think she would have done anything if she *had* seen him?"

Kent placed hands on hips and glowered at a wild rosebush near the back door. The winds off the approaching storm whipped through the trees and ushered in the smell of rain.

"Well, I, uh, guess I need to go on home before I get

drenched," Zeke said. A fat raindrop crashed into his forehead, and the sound of approaching rain propelled him to action. "See ya later," he called over his shoulder as he raced around the house toward his van. He hoped he really *did* see Kent later but somehow doubted the likelihood.

Chapter *Seven*

*T*uesday morning, Brendy dragged into the Friend-Shop at seven-thirty A.M. The store didn't open until nine, yet Brendy came in early just to have some peace. Yesterday, Kent labored a double shift, and Brendy took Pete and Pat to work with her. When the two started wrestling and knocked over a display of homemade jelly, Brendy decided to go home. She left Sylvia in charge of the store. The day went downhill from there. Pete, bent on a fight, wound up taking down the next door neighbor's son. Pat, on the other hand, refused to do anything but follow Brendy around the house all day as if she were terrified to let Brendy out of her sight. By the time Kent arrived home last night, Brendy was ready to pull her hair out.

"I'm off for a week now, Mom," Kent had said. "And you need some free time." He'd scooped the children up and headed toward the front door. On his way out, Kent called, "And just so you know, come this weekend I'm taking them to Six Flags." Pat and Pete had gone into an excited screaming fit while Kent whisked them away. Brendy had no idea where they went for the next few hours, and she was asleep when they came back home. This morning when she awoke, Brendy still experienced the overwhelming urge to escape—even though she had spent the previous evening alone.

I think I'm chronically exhausted, she mused and decided that was the only reason she could feel so draggy after ten hours of sleep. She fumbled through the walnut-stained cabinets for the raspberry mocha coffee and prepared to make her favorite brew. After spooning the grounds into the coffeemaker, Brendy folded her arms, and then rested her forehead on her fingertips. Soon, the smell of raspberries and chocolate filled the small kitchen. Brendy eyed the stainless steel appliances she scrubbed down nearly every night and wondered if she'd make it until the end of this day.

She filled her cup and meandered toward her cluttered office. As she entered, Brendy stepped over the pile of clothing she told Pete to take home yesterday. Shaking her head, Brendy wondered if her body had waited until the minute Kent took off work to flop. She also wondered about the various influences that propelled him to that decision.

Kent never mentioned what he and Zeke talked about Saturday night, and Brendy hadn't asked. *Probably me.* She took a deep swallow of her coffee, shoved back a section of wayward hair, and settled into her desk chair. A dabble of irritation marred her spirit, and she could only imagine what the two men must have said. While sneaking a peek out the back window, Brendy felt nothing short of betrayed by the both of them—as if Kent and Zeke were siding against her. After preparing that plate for Zeke, she'd been sorely tempted to take it out to him herself and set them both straight again. Nevertheless, Brendy had refused. *There's no reason to pick another fight,* she'd thought that night.

Now, Brendy wondered if she overreacted Saturday night. She had been so frazzled she wasn't certain she'd dealt rationally with the whole ordeal. By the time she tucked Pete and Pat in for the night, Brendy had still been aggravated at Zeke and Kent. Yet the brunt of her fury had been directed toward her ex-daughter-in-law.

She balled her fists. *This whole mess we're in is her*

fault! However, dwelling on the abandonment did little to relieve her fatigue. Indeed, her negative thoughts only heaped more stress upon her drained spirit.

Massaging the back of her neck, Brendy was engulfed in a cloud of loneliness, dense and unrelenting. She rearranged the folds of the denim jumper she had worn Saturday night and couldn't deny she missed Zeke— missed him as bad as she had the weeks after he left for boot camp.

The oak desk's bottom drawer was lodged open, and Brendy eyed the stack of receipts she'd dropped in last night. The edge of a keepsake box peeked from behind the pile. Brendy hadn't looked inside the box since that day two months ago when she retrieved the locket, and her heart bade her revisit the contents.

Grinding her teeth, Brendy slammed the drawer closed and turned instead to the worn Bible atop her desk. A lone dog yapped nearby as their striped cat, Tiger-Higer, sashayed into the office as if he were the king of the joint. He plopped his overstuffed self squarely in the middle of Brendy's desk and attempted to rub his face against hers. Without a smile, Brendy scratched the purring cat's ears and placed him back on the floor. She then turned to the rare treat of reading her Bible without an interruption.

But for some reason Brendy couldn't open the Word

of God today. She laid her hand upon the leather-bound book and stared at the gold letters until they blurred. Instead, all she could think of was the keepsake box in the bottom drawer. She grabbed her coffee and marched to one of the spacious windows. Brendy rested her forehead against the cool pane and stared blindly at the flower shop across the street.

Out of nowhere a gray van cruised down the street beside her shop—a gray van with "B and B Locksmith" written in black on the vehicle's door. For a wrinkle in time, Brendy thought Zeke was going to pull into her parking lot. Instead, he kept moving and never bothered even looking her way. Brendy touched the windowpane while cradling the warm coffee cup to her chest. She touched the neckline of her jumper, right where that golden locket should have been. Zeke slipped her the key Saturday night, and Brendy secretly hoped he'd planned something special for later. Something like a proposal.

She bit back a sob, and the keepsake box wouldn't be denied a moment longer. Brendy left her coffee cup on the ledge and moved toward the desk. After a hard yank on the stubborn desk drawer, she retrieved the faded symbol of her first love, opened it, and scratched through the contents until she found the tape-swathed senior ring. The green stone glistened back at her, and she remembered what Zeke had told her, "I got green because it matches your eyes," he said, explaining why he didn't choose blue, the school's color.

Tears staining her cheeks, Brendy slipped the ring in the spot her wedding band once claimed. She closed her eyes, pressed the ring to her lips, and wondered how she could have ever betrayed Zeke's pure heart. "The bad part is," she whispered, "I've done it again."

The whole worm episode rushed through her mind, and Brendy couldn't stop the impish chuckle that mingled with her tears. Pat's reaction aside, Pete's punishment had indeed fit his crime. Last night, Kent had taken a firmer hand with the child, and for the first time Brendy didn't try to interfere. She was beginning to think that maybe Zeke was right. Maybe Pete *did* need a different discipline tactic. Last night when Kent told her Pete actually stuck his tongue out at Zeke, Brendy began to doubt her methods.

A light tapping interrupted Brendy's thoughts, and she looked for Tiger-Higer, fully expecting the cat to be up to mischief. However, the feline had stretched himself out on a pile of dirty clothes and was snoozing. The tapping continued. This time, the noise sounded as if it were coming from behind her. Brendy turned to see a person peering through the window. She jumped and released a scream.

"It's just me!" Zeke called.

On second glance, Brendy recognized the man whose senior ring rested on her finger. With a rush of adrenaline, she jumped toward the window and unlatched it. The vertical pane swung outward. "You scared me to *death!*" she said, her hand upon her heart. For a moment their companionable laughter dashed aside the issues between them.

"What are you *doing*, anyway?" she asked.

"I was out on a job. When I drove by, I thought I saw you looking out the window. So I decided to stop and say, er. . ." He shuffled his boot against the pavement. "Say 'hi.'" Zeke looked back up at her, and his vulnerable expression nearly knocked her to her knees. Brendy's heart began to pound out a desperate tattoo. When Zeke's attention riveted upon the class ring still on her hand, she went breathless.

Brendy rested her fingers against the top of her coffee mug and stared at the gold ring as if it were from outer space. She hadn't put the thing on since taking it off when she met Mack.

"Ah, man," Zeke said. He shook his head and backed away.

"What?" Brendy prompted.

"Here I was, trying to act like Romeo and court you

at the window, and I see you're already *going steady.*"

She giggled and snagged her bottom lip between her teeth. The urge to apologize for Saturday night overtook her, and Brendy didn't bother to analyze the implications. "You know, Zeke," she began before she could change her mind, "I'm really sorry about blowing up on you the other night. I guess. . ." She trailed off and wondered if she were daft to try to make up.

Even if everything were resolved between her and Zeke, she still had the children to consider. Thankfully, Pat hadn't been harassed by any more bad dreams. And Pete did act a little more civilized last night after Kent took away his TV privileges for two days. Nevertheless, they still didn't like Zeke and still viewed him as a threat.

Brendy dared a glimpse at the man who had once stolen her heart. His adoring expression nearly melted her every resolve. Brendy knew she didn't look half as good as his gaze suggested. She'd barely run a comb through her hair and only applied lipstick that morning. She gulped some of her raspberry coffee and hoped the warm jolt would give her the courage to continue.

"I guess I'm just—just exhausted," she explained.

"Well, I have the perfect remedy for what ails you." He narrowed his eyes, glanced downward, and then darted a sly smile at her. "Let's get married."

Wide-eyed, Brendy looked at the man and tried to convince herself she was hearing things. "Wh–what did you—did you say?" she stuttered.

"I said, 'Let's get married,'" Zeke repeated and tugged her hand to his lips. "I can't stand being without you. And, if you want the truth, I've driven by this shop half a dozen times since yesterday. I kept telling myself I was acting like a love-struck teenager, but I can't seem to stop. This morning when I drove by, I thought it was just going to be another time to pass, but when I saw you standing in the window. . ."

A shower of tears blurred the view of the man who had always been a part of her. At once, Brendy understood part of the reason she was so exhausted after a good night's sleep. She was as lovesick as he. Brendy hadn't eaten a solid meal since Saturday night. And while Pat wasn't having any dreams about Zeke, Brendy had been haunted by images of the blue-eyed Vietnam veteran who held the key to her heart.

"We could go to Rusk this morning and get the marriage license," he continued. "You could be back at the shop by nine-thirty."

"But Sylvia doesn't get here until ten, and the shop opens at nine." Brendy felt as if her head were spinning with details.

"So, put a note on the door that you'll be here at nine-thirty."

"But what about Mr. Narvy and—"

"They can wait," Zeke said. "All they're going to do is sit around and play checkers until lunch anyway."

"This is crazy," Brendy said. She tugged her hand from his and deposited her coffee on the windowsill once more.

"No, it's not." Zeke placed his hands on the window-pane and leaned toward her. Given the elevation of the hardwood floor, Brendy stood eye-to-eye with Zeke. "It's not crazy," he said. "It's love."

His face neared hers, and Brendy was drawn by the magnetism that had reignited the moment Ziggy Blake stepped back into her life. Common sense issued two suggestions. First, Brendy shouldn't kiss him because a kiss would signify their relationship was back in swing. Second, if that officially happened she would again be facing choices that affected her grandchildren.

Nevertheless, Brendy couldn't resist the thought of Zeke's lips upon hers. Not only did she let him kiss her, she kissed him back. She flung her arms around his neck and kissed him with the abandon of a woman irrevocably in love.

As he trailed a row of kisses toward her ear, Brendy

whispered, "Kent says he's taking the kids to Six Flags this weekend," and didn't bother to expound upon her meaning.

"If we get the license today, we can get married Friday. We'd have the whole weekend together—*alone.*" Zeke sounded as if he'd been given a pot of gold.

"But what are we going to do once they get home?" she worried.

"I don't have the foggiest idea," Zeke answered.

He followed that with a kiss that left Brendy without recollection of her own name. And within fifteen minutes she found herself being whisked away to the Cherokee County Courthouse, thinking they were indeed crazy or this was what her daughter called a "Godthing."

Chapter *Eight*

From Tuesday until Friday Zeke felt as if he were caught up in a whirlwind of expectation, plans, and mystery. The expectation nearly rivaled his emotions when he and Brendy had talked of getting married the first time. His plans involved getting his best suit cleaned and picking up the set of matching gold bands from the jewelers.

Brendy's plans, however, proved more complicated. Indeed, Zeke only got a few minutes alone with her between her flitting all over town. According to Sylvia, her plans involved getting her hair and nails done at Rainbow's End, or arranging a makeover with Debbie and Cheryl at Merle Norman Cosmetics, or purchasing the perfect suit from Elaine's. How she kept their wedding a secret in a town as small as Jacksonville was a mystery to Zeke.

By the time he picked her up Friday evening at five of six, Zeke decided all her preparation had been worth it. "You look great," he whispered as he helped her into the front seat of his van. Her jade green, two-piece suit made her hair appear as if it were on fire—a fire that matched the blaze in Zeke's veins. "And you smell great too," he added before placing a lingering kiss on her lips.

"Mmmm," she purred, "it's Shalimar."

"I know. I would recognize that scent from ten miles away," he said. "You're wearing your locket?" he asked and glanced toward her neck.

She touched the gold heart and smiled. "You have the key?"

He pulled the tiny key from his suit pocket and held it up for her inspection.

"I guess we're all set, then," she said.

"Yes, all set," Zeke said and wanted to stand and look at her until the sun set and they were surrounded by shadows that resonated with their love. But, alas, the Reverend Crandall Henderson was awaiting them at First Church on the corner of Beaumont and Bryan Streets.

Within half an hour they would be husband and wife. Zeke had planned for a private meal to be catered at his home. After that, he hoped they could come back to her place and spend the weekend in marital bliss. What they would do when the kids came home was still an enigma. Neither of them spoke of that problem. As he climbed into the van, Zeke sensed they had somehow made a silent pact to enjoy the weekend and let tomorrow take care of its problems.

Five minutes later, Brendy and Zeke stepped along the sidewalk of the small church he attended. They passed a bed of multicolored impatiens and begonias before Zeke tried the glass door. When he tugged on the handle, the door didn't budge. He frowned, cupped his hands, and gazed into the modest foyer. Only the whir of intermittent traffic bespoke any activity.

"No sign of life," he muttered and wondered what they would do if his pastor forgot. He was known for his "absentminded professor" syndrome, and Zeke checked his watch. "Six o'clock on the dot," he said. "We're right on time."

"What if he forgot?" Brendy asked, and her voice wobbled.

Zeke turned toward her, covered her hands with his, and couldn't deny the tremor in her fingers. "You're nervous," he said and searched her guileless gaze for any hint of uncertainty. All he saw was excitement.

"And you're not?" she provoked with a flirtatious smile.

"Nervous? Me? Not in the least," he teased, and Brendy laughed. Zeke tugged on the stifling neck of his starched white shirt. He couldn't deny that his perspiration was as much from nerves as July humidity.

"Look, let's walk around the church," Zeke added. "The side door is often left open. The pastor lives right next door. Maybe you can at least go in and sit in the cool while I see if I can find him."

Brendy walked around the church with Zeke, and they discovered the side door open, just as he predicted. He ushered her in, flipped on the lights, and promised to be back with the absentee minister. Once Zeke closed the door and Brendy had the cozy sanctuary to herself, she thrilled in the holy silence.

Sunlight streamed through the stained glass windows, creating a feeling of walking inside a rainbow. A large vase filled with eucalyptus and dried flowers stood on a table behind the altar. The smell of hymnals and carpet deodorizer tinged her senses as Brendy moved toward the flowers.

Near the vase, she touched the pages of an open Bible. The displayed passages were from Jeremiah, chapter twenty-nine. An unknown hand had underlined verse eleven. " 'For I know the plans I have for you,' declares the Lord, 'plans to prosper you and not to harm you, plans to give you hope and a future.' "

Brendy considered the whirlwind of activity since she'd recklessly accepted Zeke's proposal. Her sneaky shopping had led up to Kent's departure that afternoon. He had driven off with the kids chanting, "Six Flags! Six Flags! Six Flags!" She only hoped Kent could maintain his new upbeat persona once he realized his mom had gotten married behind his back.

She moved to the altar and knelt. Her knees cracked as they touched the short-piled carpet, and Brendy was reminded she was no longer a carefree eighteen year old. Nevertheless, her soul soared with the hope of a rewarding marriage. And the words from Jeremiah 29:11 became her own. Slowly, she placed her hands upon the altar and rested her forehead upon her hands. A prayer sprang from her heart: thankfulness for the gift of Zeke, petition for her son and grandchildren, joy for her place in God's love.

Upon the heels of her thanksgiving, a tender voice nudged her to also pray for her ex-daughter-in-law. Brendy stiffened. Her head rose, and she gripped the edge of the altar. Thoughts of that fickle female nearly banished all Brendy's joy. Even though she had often said something like, "All we can do is pray for her," the words were a mere sentiment. For she seriously struggled with speaking a sincere prayer for the betterment of the woman who had abandoned those innocent children.

The men's footsteps nearing the side door banished the moment. Relieved, Brendy stood from the altar and watched Zeke enter with the portly pastor.

"I don't know why, but I put this wedding on my schedule for six-thirty," Reverend Henderson was saying as they came in.

"No problem," Zeke acquiesced. "I understand. You have a busy schedule. We're just thankful you could perform the ceremony on such short notice."

The reverend slowed as he neared Brendy. The two had met numerous times around town, and she welcomed the handshake of the kind minister. "I always say the smartest men are the ones who marry higher than themselves." The fiftyish pastor smiled at Zeke. "Looks like you're probably about the smartest man I've met."

Brendy warmed and Zeke offered a jovial protest.

"I guess I should say, aside from me," Henderson added. "I somehow managed to marry a woman twelve years younger than I. She's tall and blond and way prettier than I am. It's nothing short of a miracle." He rubbed the top of his balding head and chuckled.

After the humorous exchange, Reverend Henderson suggested the three of them hold hands and pray. Brendy marveled at the presence of the Lord as the skilled pastor closed the prayer and began the ceremony, keeping it brief yet meaningful.

As they exchanged wedding bands, the years melted away, and Brendy felt as if they were standing beneath that weeping willow tree on Lake Jacksonville. The summer sun still glistened across the water like a shower of glitter. Brendy wasn't so certain she didn't hear the mockingbird's sweet song, and she could almost smell the fresh summer breeze whispering through the weeping willow.

Finally, the pastor spoke the long-awaited words, "I now pronounce you husband and wife." Brendy beamed up at her handsome husband as the minister added, "I understand the two of you have something special you'd like to do now."

"Yes." Zeke pulled a key from his suit pocket as Brendy fumbled with the locket's clasp. After removing the chain the two of them worked to unlock the tiny heart that had been closed over thirty years before. At last, the spring released and they gazed upon a diminutive black-and-white photo of themselves. They were sitting upon the hood of Zeke's black Mustang and smiling with the cheerful assurance that the future was nothing but bright.

Yet that photo had been taken before the cruelties of Vietnam. . .before loss. . .before the heartaches of life.

As if the locket released the essence of their first love, Brendy felt as if she were swept away in a tide only matched by that moment when Zeke first kissed her. As if he too were whisked into the waves of first love, Zeke pulled Brendy close and didn't wait for the minister to tell him to kiss his bride. She threw her arms around his neck and pressed her lips against his with the enthusiasm of a married woman.

The enthusiasm increased as the night progressed, through the catered candlelit meal, during the time they softly swayed to the music in Zeke's living room, all the way to the moment they pulled into Brendy's driveway.

The weekend blurred into a home-based honeymoon that left Brendy's head spinning and raised the eyebrows of a few neighbors. Finally, she was forced to tell their next-door neighbor that she and Zeke had secretively wed. Otherwise, she didn't think her reputation would have remained intact another two days.

By Saturday night around nine-thirty, the two love-birds decided what they needed now was a good night's rest. Kent was due home Sunday by supper, and both Brendy and Zeke were stressed with how to share the news of their marriage. While Zeke suggested the bold approach, Brendy thought they ought to keep a low profile for as many weeks as possible.

After brushing her teeth and running her hairbrush through her curls, Brendy snapped off the bathroom light and glided toward the four-poster bed. She'd taken special pains to enhance the room's classic Victorian atmosphere, so they each felt more like they were at a bed-and-breakfast than at her home. The smell of the butter-cream candle that had burned most of last night still clung to the air. And Brendy suspected she would never smell butter-cream again without thinking of the night that she and Zeke fulfilled the dreams of over three decades.

Zeke, stretched on his back, observed her through heavy lids. He had the covers pulled up to his chin, and Brendy snickered. "Still trying to hide those threadbare pajamas?" she asked and slipped out of the silky robe that covered her sensational peach negligee trimmed in Belgian lace. Last night Zeke had told her she resembled a queen.

"Well, compared to *your* nightclothes, I look like a vagabond," he admitted with a roll of his eyes. "I guess I needed a coach for this wedding thing. I was in Beall's department store Thursday working on their security equipment. I could have bought a whole drawer full of pajamas, but it never even crossed my mind."

"That's okay, Honey," Brendy soothed. "I love you even though you *do* wear pink pajamas." She clicked off the lamp, and a nearby streetlamp filled the room with an unforgettable luminescence.

"Now she's mocking me," Zeke teased as Brendy slid against the cool sheets. "They're not pink! They're *red*," he insisted. "Or they were when I bought them!"

Brendy giggled and settled her head against his shoulder. His hand descended upon her curls, and his fingers lovingly caressed her forehead. "And when was that?" she asked with a honey-sweet tone, *"1975?"*

"Well, I oughta—" Zeke raised up on his elbow and began tickling her tummy.

With a delightful squeal, Brendy tried to squirm away, but to no avail. Finally, she grabbed the only defense she could clutch and whacked him over the head with her pillow.

"Ugh!" he croaked and clutched his chest. "She got me!" He flopped onto his back, and the laughter of two souls knit as one spun a musical chant into the room.

He tugged her close again, and Brendy settled her head upon his shoulder. "I love you, Ziggy Blake," she whispered.

"And I love you," he echoed. "I wish—" He halted, and Brendy waited for him to finish.

Chapter Nine

Finally, she propped herself up on one elbow and scrutinized his profile. Brendy rested a hand against those infamous pink pajamas and finally said, "You wish?"

"How do I say this?" His eyes glistened in the streetlamp's silvery highlights, and Brendy expected he was grappling for words. At last, Zeke propped his hand under his head and looked straight at her. "Can I be honest?" he asked.

"Of course." Brendy stroked the side of his face and took in the faint scent of Brut. She would go to her grave loving that stuff.

"Okay," Zeke finally said like a brave soldier. "Let's

see how we survive brutal honesty."

"Shoot," she encouraged.

"I. . .hmm. . .how do I say this?"

"Just *say* it!" she encouraged. "Say it or I'll go insane!" Brendy touched her temple.

"Right. Well, you asked for it, then. I. . .already know that you and I have something Madeline and I never had." Zeke's words reverberated around the room like a phantom of the past. "I was going to say I wish I could have had this kind of marriage with her, but then that sounded *really stupid*. So, I started to say I wish I'd married *you* in the first place, but—"

"But that was a decision I made for both of us," Brendy inserted, and she couldn't keep the regret from marring every word.

"That's *not* what I was going to say," Zeke insisted. "I was going to say that if I hadn't married Maddy, then I wouldn't have my sons, and I can't imagine life without them."

"Did you call them about our marriage?" Brendy asked, ready to grab at any diversion from the well of guilt springing from her soul. Strangely, amid the guilt came thoughts of her daughter-in-law.

"Actually, yes."

"I still haven't even met them," she said and tried to

force all images of that vixen from her mind.

"They're in shock," he admitted.

"I wonder if they'll like me."

"Who knows? I'm certainly not winning any popularity contest with *your* relatives, so. . ."

"I told my mother this morning," Brendy continued. Somehow, she hoped the repartee would extinguish the humiliating conviction from her spirit that grew the longer she pondered her daughter-in-law. For the first time, Brendy was faced with the fact that she had done to Zeke what her ex-daughter-in-law had done to Kent and the kids. And Brendy had yet to forgive her—truly forgive her. *But I'd never leave my children,* she argued. Nevertheless, the still small voice that urged her to pray for Tamela now insisted *Brendy* had also violated a promise that broke a man's heart.

A realization hit her smack between the eyes. She had allowed herself to think the name *Tamela* for the first time since Kent and Tamela's ugly divorce. Brendy had been so hurt by what that woman did she hadn't even wanted to hear her name.

Now the mere echo of the word. . .*Tamela*. . .ushered in a holy comparison—a comparison of Brendy's betrayal of Zeke with Tamela's betrayal of Kent. *But we weren't married,* she thought and wanted to shrink from sight under the fragrant sheets. Even so, Brendy knew she couldn't escape the reality. She had broken a promise that ripped out a man's heart. *How can I hold a grudge against Tamela?* Brendy wrestled with the intrusive thought and wished she could escape the brutal truth.

"Zeke?" she whispered.

"Hmm?" he asked.

"I'm sorry."

She hadn't realized he was tense until his arm relaxed against her shoulder. "What for?" he crooned and stroked her hair again. "Here I was worried you were angry, and—"

"No, not angry in the least," Brendy said, her voice cracking. "I just. . ." She sniffled.

"Hey." Zeke rose to his elbow. "Why all the tears?" he asked, his face only inches from hers.

"I'm just so sorry about—about jilting you," she admitted. "And I'm not sure I ever even told you—not until now."

"It doesn't even matter. I forgave you years ago. As a matter of fact—" He stopped again.

Sensing his hesitancy once more, Brendy laid a hand on his face. "Go ahead. We might as well tell all," she encouraged.

"Well, Maddy and I didn't have what you and I have," he admitted, "but she *needed* me, Brendy. Her father was a drunk who beat her half to death. Her mother didn't do a thing to stop him. By the time I met her, she had somehow managed to struggle through licensed vocational nursing school and was pretty much an emotional version of my physical problems. The two of us together were a wreck, I can assure you. I think maybe that's what attracted us to each other. We were both pretty much chewed up, but we had somehow managed to survive." Zeke settled back onto his pillow. "Or I guess *I* survived better than she did."

Brendy rested her hand under her head and watched the shadows chase across the ceiling as a car cruised down the dark street. She grappled for any words to help ease the forlorn echo in his voice, but nothing came. Finally, Brendy said, "I don't know what to say."

"I didn't tell you the whole story of her death, Brendy, because, well. . ." Zeke shifted under the covers, and Brendy looked at him through the shadows. He placed his forefinger and thumb against his eyes, and her pulse responded to his anguish. "She committed suicide," Zeke finally blurted. "I came home one day from work, and she'd done the old car-in-the-closed-garage routine."

"Oh, no!" Brendy gasped and her eyes stung. "Oh, Zeke. I–I'm so sorry."

"It was a couple of years after our sons left for college. She wrestled with depression most of our married life. I think she just couldn't handle the fact that they were gone—for good."

Brendy laid a hand on his chest and pressed her lips against his cheek. She came away with a trace of dampness and salt.

"Really, Brendy," he continued, and she marveled that his voice revealed little sign of tears, "I've spent the last five years hurting because I—I somehow think I failed her. I'm not sure my sons are over it all either—"

"I don't see how they ever *could* be."

"I hope you'll be patient with them. They both hinted that they thought you might be after my nest egg."

Brendy laughed outright and rolled toward him.

"That was my exact reaction. I think it aggravated both of 'em. I'll tell you what, people who don't have identical twins just don't know what they're missing. What one thinks, the other one thinks. You just might as well get ready for it." He shook his head.

"I guess the Lord has brought both of us through a lot, huh?" she asked.

"Seems that way," Zeke agreed. His arm slipped around her once more and pulled her closer. Brendy reveled in the security he emanated. Already, she loved being the wife of Ezekiel Blake.

The sound of summer crickets singing the joys of night ushered in a hush between the newlyweds. A hush that took Brendy back to the altar of that church where they married. Back to the point of praying for Tamela. Back to the point of realizing that she was no better than Tamela. Nevertheless, her chest tightened with the mere thought of what the woman had done to Brendy's son and grandchildren.

"Ziggy," she finally said, accompanied by the distant siren of an ambulance. "I need you to pray for me."

"Oh?"

"Yes. I, uh. . ." Brendy swallowed. "I'm having trouble forgiving Tamela."

"Who?"

"Tamela. Kent's ex-wife."

"I can't imagine why," he said with a twist of irony.

Brendy thanked God that her husband understood as she continued her explanation. "It would appear that the Lord is showing me I'm no better than she is. I abandoned *you*. Now, how can I hold a grudge against Tamela?" She balled the freshly laundered sheet in her hand. "But it's still so hard to release the pain."

Zeke remained silent, and Brendy wondered what he might be thinking. At last he said, "I know from experience that sometimes forgiveness comes in layers—kinda like an onion. Right now, you've come to the first step of realizing the need to forgive. From here, it's all about releasing the memory to God every time it comes to your mind and allowing Him to heal your hurt until He takes the healing all the way to the core. For some people that takes several years; for others, it's more of a deliverance."

"You sound like you've done this." Tears seeped from her eyes, for she already knew the answer.

"I have," he said, and the rumble of truth vibrated against her cheek resting upon his chest. "I was one of the slower ones," he admitted.

"That would be. . .when you forgave me?" she asked.

He stroked her cheek with his thumb. "That would be. . .when I forgave you," Zeke affirmed.

Brendy wrapped her arms around her husband and held on tight. *Oh, Jesus*, she finally prayed, *teach me to forgive Tamela like Zeke forgave me.* The instant the words left her heart, a warm assurance flowed into Brendy's soul. For the first time in months she rested—truly rested—in the presence of a holy God.

Brendy didn't have all the answers. And she wasn't about to pretend she would stop hurting for her grandchildren. Nevertheless, she knew God had heard her prayer and was beginning to answer in His own way, in His own time. He had heard and was extending to Brendy the desire to begin praying for Tamela, and Brendy would—for her own spiritual well-being.

The sound of a car pulling into the driveway pierced the moment with a hint of intrigue. Zeke stiffened. Brendy clutched his arm. They looked at each other, nose-to-nose, through the shadows.

"When was Kent supposed to be home again?" he whispered.

"Not until tomorrow evening—around dinner," Brendy hissed back.

A car door slammed. The ebb and flow of children's voices preceded the clatter and creak of the front door being opened.

"Oh, my word," Brendy said, "he's brought them home early! What are we going to do?"

"Look, maybe they won't even suspect I'm here," Zeke reasoned.

"Are you *kidding!*" Brendy shot back. "Your van is parked at the curb."

Zeke groaned. "My van. How could I have forgotten?"

"Grandmom!" Pat's shrill voice floated up the hallway.

"Mom? Zeke?" Kent called. "They've got to be here somewhere," he mumbled as he neared the bedroom.

"Zeke's van is at the curb."

"Maybe they went somewhere in Grandmom's van," Pete said, and his words dripped disapproval.

"Her van is in the driveway," Kent answered, and his voice now held a hint of concern. "I hope there hasn't been an emergency." A hesitant knock reverberated upon her door. "Mom?" Kent called. "Are you in there? Is everything okay?"

Brendy gulped in a decisive breath and snapped on the lamp.

"Might as well face the music," Zeke mumbled.

"Brace yourself," Brendy said with a wince.

The two partners exchanged a flash of silent communication and simultaneously nodded as if they were preparing to head into the most fiendish of enemy fire.

"Come in," they said in unison.

Chapter *Ten*

*A*s the door swished open, Kent gaped at his mom as if she were the most wanton of women. Brendy held up her left hand to display the wide gold band. Zeke followed suit.

"We're married," they said together.

"Married!" Kent yelped. By that time, two tired faces, smeared with candied apple, appeared behind their dad. "When?" he demanded.

"Last night," Brendy said. "After you left."

Pete clutched his father's arm and gazed at Zeke as if he were a space alien. Bursting into a wail, Pat reached for Kent. He scooped her into his arms while keeping a firm hand upon Pete's shoulder. Pat snuggled against her father's neck and reduced her crying to whimpers.

Holding her breath, Brendy counted the seconds until the inevitable explosion. Yet no explosion came. Only silence. Silence and relief. Relief and a new realization. With her own eyes, Brendy watched as Kent's children turned to him for solace rather than insisting upon her.

"Well!" Kent finally said, and his full lips twisted. "I guess you two really pulled one over on *me.*"

"Uh. . . ," Brendy started and looked to Zeke.

"We. . . ," Zeke began and glanced at Brendy.

"An apology might be in order," Kent huffed as if he were Brendy's offended father. "The kids wanted to come home early because we thought you might be lonely!"

Pete glared at Zeke. Brendy, tense and ready for anything, noticed Zeke wasn't flinching from the child's hostile stare.

"Does Grandmother know?" Kent asked.

"Yes. I called her this morning," Brendy explained.

"So I'm the last to know?" His brown eyes rounded, and the dark circles beneath matched the tired state of his T-shirt and pleated shorts.

"No, I still haven't told Leandra," Brendy admitted, referring to her daughter.

"I'm sure *she's* going to be thrilled to be the last to

know." Kent settled onto the end of the bed, lowered Pat to his leg, and pulled Pete into the circle of his arm. "This is just *too weird,*" Kent mumbled. "The last I knew, worms were flying around the dining room table, and you guys weren't speaking."

"Well, I guess we just realized that nothing could keep us apart." Zeke cut a humorous glance toward Brendy. "Not even worms," he added.

Kent's tired chuckle seemed to relieve his aggravation.

"I don't like worms." With a shiver, Pat covered her mouth. She reached for Brendy, who gathered the child into her arms.

Zeke stroked the little girl's hair, and she didn't flinch from his touch. "I wouldn't have put a worm in your mouth the other night, Sweetie," he said. "And I was just fooling around with Pete. I didn't mean for that worm to fall in."

Pat eyed Zeke as if she might want to believe him.

"I missed you, Grandmom," she finally claimed, and Brendy lifted a brow as she pieced together the rest of the reason they'd come home early. "Can I sleep with you tonight?" Pat asked.

"Of course," Zeke answered before anyone else could.

"But—" Kent started.

"We don't have to—" Brendy began.

Zeke held up his hand. "Now that I'm a part of this family, we might as well act like it."

"She snores," Brendy mumbled.

"Put her over there on the other side of you, and I'll never know it," Zeke said with the gallant air of an honorable knight.

"Oh, and one more thing." He turned to Pete, who didn't offer even the hint of a smile. "I left that shopping bag here the other night. Your grandmother told me she put it in the top of the hall closet. There's a ball glove in there for you, if you want it, and I really like to play catch."

Pete looked down. And while he offered no acceptance, neither did he reject the idea.

Kent extended his hand to his new stepfather. "You're all right," he said as the two men shook hands.

"So are you," Zeke responded, and Brendy covered their hands with hers.